# FAITH *in the* POOR

# TO LUCAS

*May he always have faith
but never be poor*

# FAITH *in the* POOR

### B O B   H O L M A N

A LION BOOK

Copyright © Bob Holman

The author asserts the moral right
to be identified as the author of this work

Published by
**Lion Publishing plc**
Sandy Lane West, Oxford, England
ISBN 0 7459 3991 0

First edition 1998
10 9 8 7 6 5 4 3 2 1 0

**Acknowledgments**
Unless otherwise stated, the biblical references in this book
are taken from the Good News Bible.

A catalogue record for this book is available
from the British Library

Typeset in 12.5/15 Bembo
Printed and bound in Great Britain by
Biddles Ltd, Guildford and King's Lynn

# Contents

Part 1 – The Wrong Writers      7

Part 2 – The Right Writers      29

    *Carol*      29

    *Bill*      50

    *Erica*      56

    *Anita*      79

    *Denise*      104

    *Penny*      110

    *Cynthia*      124

Part 3 – Faith in the Poor      153

Bibliography      219

# Part 1

# The Wrong Writers

Easterhouse is a huge housing scheme, with a population of around 40,000, on the edge of Glasgow. Books have been written about the place and its people. It often features in newspaper articles and TV reports. Much of what is published conveys Easterhouse in negative terms. An academic analysis of Easterhouse, published in 1985, stated:

> Situated four to five miles north-east of the centre of Glasgow, Easterhouse is one of the city's four major peripheral council estates, which were developed during the 1950s as part of the city's slum clearance and overspill programme... From the start it had a large proportion of households in urgent need of accommodation, many large families, and a high proportion of working class households. Problems increased rapidly, compounded by the relative inaccessibility of employment opportunities in the city and the chronic lack of local services... it quickly became known as a 'problem area', with widely publicized youthful delinquency and

vandalism. It was not long before problems of construction, repair and maintenance of even this relatively new housing stock began to multiply, exacerbating the already poor environmental and social conditions. The sheer scale of Easterhouse contributed further to its poor visual image and reputation as a deprived area…Vandalism, crime, and the much publicized problems of anti-social behaviour among school pupils are all part of Easterhouse's reputation. As the city's population has declined, many Easterhouse residents who can exercise a choice – often the better off, or more stable, maturer households – want to leave. Easterhouse exhibits all the signs of its low income – low car ownership, problems of rent arrears and fuel disconnections, lack of commercial entertainment centres, and a narrow range of shops.[1]

In the 1990s, the American guru Charles Murray came to Britain to expand his view that a growing underclass of inadequate, immoral, work-shy people was threatening the stability and prosperity of Britain. His book, sponsored by *The Sunday Times* and the Institute of Economic Affairs, declared that the underclass was largely made up of two groupings, 'young, healthy, low income males [who] choose not to take jobs' and single mothers who choose to have children outside of stable relationships. He asserted that the bored men turned to crime and drugs while the feckless women neglected their children, who became the next generation of criminal layabouts. Poverty, unemployment, the decline in sexual behaviour was thus largely attributed to the personal inadequacies of the underclass, to their immorality, their rejection of the work ethic, their abandonment of the traditional family, and their lack of abilities. Following a brief visit, Murray concluded that Easterhouse was an example of the underclass. He told an anecdote he had heard about the unwillingness of Easterhouse young men to take jobs. He compared Easterhouse to inner city New York calling them 'communities without fathers [where] the kids tend to run wild'.[2]

Numerous newspaper articles have followed the same themes. The well-known writer, Alan Massie, in a piece in the Glasgow *Herald*, took Easterhouse as representative of Scotland's urban problems and continued, 'the word Easterhouse represents failure, deprivation, poverty and squalor. Would anyone live there of choice?'[3] In a long article in *The Observer*, David Harrison described the flat of an Easterhouse resident:

Mary McLeish doesn't notice the peeling paint and graffiti in the entrance hall to her Glasgow flat any more. Inside, she points almost matter-of-factly to the damp on her bedroom wall, six inches from her pillow, still there after 11 years, despite numerous pleas to the council. In the living room the 65-year-old widow shrugs stoically when she tries to open the window and the frame comes away from the wall. This is one of the better flats on the notorious Easterhouse estate where drugs, crime and unemployment are all rife... One senior Glasgow academic suggested last week that Easterhouse should be demolished and the residents scattered throughout Glasgow.[4]

The article was accompanied by a large photograph of an abandoned tenement block with the heading, 'Drug dealers, vandals, crumbling buildings – but some call it home.'

It is not to be denied that Easterhouse has many social deprivations compared with most other parts of Britain. Professor Michael Pacione uses census data to point out that within it, between 1981 and 1991, male unemployment increased from 35.1 per cent to 44.8 per cent, that female unemployment rose from 19.2 per cent to 30.6 per cent, while the proportion of households without cars remained almost static at 81.9 per cent. He added that deaths in the first year of life in Easterhouse were 46.7 per 1000 compared with 10.0 per 1000 in the nearby middle class suburb of Bishopbriggs.[5] The anger felt by many Easterhouse residents is not with the statement of facts like these. It is rather that writers tend to be economical with the truth. They do not emphasize that a majority of eligible adults are in employment, that over 70 per cent of children are in two-parent households, that some council housing has been improved, while the type of housing stock has been widened by private building, housing associations and housing co-operatives. In particular, they are aggrieved that so little mention is made of the hundreds of locally run voluntary bodies which thrive in the area.

The misrepresentation by writers has serious

consequences. It adds to the wrong image of Easterhouse. Recently, a reporter from a national newspaper flew to Glasgow to cover the story that the Easterhouse police were to be armed with CS sprays. At the airport, he found the taxi driver reluctant to drive to Easterhouse for fear of what would happen to him and the taxi. In actuality, they arrived with no trouble and the reporter was set down in a quiet and pleasant street. He was then taken to a local project where he met residents who were objecting to the selection of Easterhouse as the location for a pilot study for CS sprays. They pointed out that the area's crime figures were no worse than many other places: but Easterhouse has a press image of being 'notorious'. The image also serves to hinder investment in Easterhouse. It contains many empty factories and warehouses which are within yards of the motorway, but firms are reluctant to fill them. The council offered favourable terms to a company to build a cinema complex in Easterhouse. It went elsewhere. Young people complain that their job applications have less chance because they live in Easterhouse. Not least, the bad press gives credence to the views that Easterhouse is overrun by an underclass.

## The wrong writers

The unbalanced image of Easterhouse arises because the articles are too often by the wrong writers. They are by outsiders not by residents. They are by journalists – and sometimes by academics – who make brief forays into Easterhouse. During these visits they concentrate on a negative aspect – they spotlight a death related to drug abuse but do not mention the many local teenagers who shun drugs; they give details of a violent crime but do not mention the many law-abiding citizens; they portray the loan sharks but not the locally run credit unions. Journalists do not want balance. When the Social Justice Commission visited Easterhouse, it was accompanied by a photographer from a national paper. I asked him to take pictures of the newly renovated flats. He smiled, agreed to snap both decaying and refurbished housing and added, 'But I can guarantee which one will appear.' He was right; the editor chose a photo which implied that all of Easterhouse was a slum. A TV researcher came prior to some news coverage on Easterhouse; he met some local families, all depending upon Income Support, all of whom had tidy homes with carpets or lino on the floor. 'This is no good', he complained. 'I want a family living on the floorboards. Real poverty.' I asked him how much he earned. It emerged that he and his partner had a combined income of £80,000 compared with under £10,000 for the local families. I suggested the news item should concentrate on inequality not poverty. He dismissed the idea. As a rich outsider, he did not want that kind of coverage.

Easterhouse residents do sometimes try to counter their bad press. In 1993, a local activist wrote to a newspaper following an article which had concentrated on the Easterhouse drug abusers, alcoholics and criminals. The editor refused to publish an immediate disclaimer but suggested the activist call a meeting of people involved in the positive side of Easterhouse. He did so and gathered together representatives of housing associations, housing co-operatives, credit unions, neighbourhood centres, the Citizens Advice Bureau, an elderly people's forum and other groups. The members then compiled an article about the good things in Easterhouse. The editor declined to publish on the grounds that it was not newsworthy. The example represents a difficulty faced by Easterhouse and its residents. It is not that Easterhouse contains no positive features. It is not that local residents cannot write. The problem is that their efforts cannot get national publication.

## The top-down approach

The difficulty is not confined to Easterhouse. The British media has a top-down approach to the coverage of items of social deprivation. *The Guardian*, more than most newspapers, is sympathetic towards people with low incomes. Yet it rarely allows poor people to write. Instead columnists, who are socially and geographically distanced from life at the hard end, write about the poor. When *The Guardian* published an eight-page supplement on the budget, there were comments from sixty-two contributors, from well-paid journalists, from Oxbridge economists, from seven wise and wealthy women and seven wise and powerful men. Yet not one sentence was written by the residents of peripheral estates, although their lives were markedly affected by the budget. When *The Observer* in 1997 devoted much of one edition to poverty, the poor were not allowed to contribute one word. Indeed, the major piece was written by Roy Hattersley. As an MP, Hattersley's earnings were £100,000 a year. Now he is Lord Hattersley. In other words, it was the very rich and the very privileged writing about the very poor. Similarly, the *New Statesman & Society* is considered a radical journal but the majority of its contributors have the same privileged backgrounds and lifestyles as other leading writers. This is not to say that able journalists fail to criticize governments for not tackling poverty. It is to say that even the left-of-centre papers exclude any expression by people with low incomes just as much as *The Daily Telegraph* or *The Sunday Times*.

It is not just the written word. Consider *Question Time*, BBC TV's main forum for public debate. In 1983 and 1993, I made an analysis of the membership of the panels in this programme. Participants were overwhelmingly made up of politicians, journalists, heads of large organizations and quangos. They were likely to be wealthy, powerful, mainly from the southern establishment and listed in *Who's Who*. The same kind of people appeared on radio's *Any Questions*.[6] Of course, the panellists did have views worth listening to. But completely excluded were low wage earners, those dependent upon giro cheques, residents of the inner cities, and tenants of council flats.

In 1996, Channel 4 TV made the brave decision to broadcast a series of programmes about poverty, under the title *Broke*. Programmes showed the shaky foundations of the economy and explained how the dominance of the free market had escalated unemployment and poverty. Other documentaries featured the plight of drug abusers, of abandoned youngsters, of the victims of loan sharks. Yet the presenters of the programmes were always the affluent and well-bred. Poor people were portrayed, occasionally interviewed to illustrate a point, but they were kept from any control over what was said. Their views counted for nothing. The prevailing attitude was well expressed by John Perry, chief policy officer of the Chartered Institute of Housing, when he stated that working class areas have become weaker because private housing in the country 'serves to draw articulate middle-class people out of the cities'.[7] The implication is that working-class people are inarticulate and cannot cope without their middle-class betters.

Will Hutton has explained that Britain is a 40–30–30 society. At the top are the 40 per cent who enjoy high salaries, secure employment, large homes and are increasingly identifying with private systems of education, health and pensions. The middle 30 per cent have moderate incomes, probably own semi-detached houses, have holidays abroad. The bottom 30 per cent are dependent upon low wages or welfare benefits, rely upon deteriorating public services and tend to dwell in the inner cities and peripheral housing estates.[8] In terms of public communication and expression, it is the words and voices of the top 40 per cent – supplemented by the middle 30 per cent – which are read and heard. Those of the bottom 30 per cent are silenced.

The exclusion from the national media of the 'forgotten 30 per cent' has four serious outcomes. One, as already indicated, is that topics like poverty, inequality, social deprivations, life on estates, are seen only through the perspectives and interpretations of outsiders, of those whose incomes and lifestyles are as socially removed from those who experience them as Mars is from the earth.

The second is that the reluctance to listen to the bottom 30 per cent serves to devalue them. They are seen as inferiors who, at best, might write for community papers with small circulations but who must leave the nationals to their superiors. With regard to social topics, they are treated as specimens to be examined and displayed, not as human beings with the rights and capacities to participate in public debate.

The third is that the process lends weight to the underclass or 'blame the poor' mentality. They are kept from having any weight in newspapers and broadcasting because they are deemed to be too unintelligent and too inarticulate to make worthwhile contributions. In short, they are to blame for their silence just as they are to blame for their poverty.

The fourth is that the system contributes to the maintenance of inequality. As I have tried to explain elsewhere, inequality is not an accident. Inequality is determined and maintained by complex economic and social mechanisms. The silencing of the bottom 30 per cent lessens the challenge to the *status quo*. 'Thus power in the media is exploited to ensure that the views and interests of the privileged are conveyed while those of the deprived are neglected.'[9]

## A Christian perspective

Poor people are excluded from public expression of their views in the media. So what? Similarly it might be asked, why bother that 30 per cent of the population have to endure much lower standards of health, accommodation, education, job prospects and so on than the rest of the population? Those who are concerned may draw their reasons and values from various political, religious and humanistic beliefs. My core beliefs and practices are drawn from Christianity, and hence it is appropriate, at this stage, that I set down why I consider Christians should be opposed to the exclusion of a sizeable number of citizens from mainstream British life.

I start with the biblical basis about creation. In Genesis, it is recorded, 'So God created human beings, making them to be like himself. He created them male and female, blessed them and said, "Have many children, so that your descendants will live all over the earth and bring it under their control"' (Genesis 1:27). If God made human beings 'to be like himself' then all individuals must be of enormous value. If God chose to shape them, as the Authorized Version puts it, 'in his own image', then he must consider everyone to be of great importance, and it follows that the created should also regard their fellow creatures as of immense value.

Further, it is clear that God created people equal with each other. He did not make them as royals and subjects, as aristocrats and commoners, as masters and slaves, as superiors and inferiors. As the great Christian socialist, R.H. Tawney concluded, 'The necessary corollary of the Christian conception of man is a strong sense of equality.

Equality does not mean that all men are equally clever or equally tall or equally fat. It means that all... are of equal value.'[10] Significantly, God commissioned all people to control and benefit from the earth. He did not decree that 40 per cent should possess most, 30 per cent a good slice, and 30 per cent very little. The earth was made the responsibility of all and for the good of all. From the very start there was an equality about the value of human beings, about their relationships with each other, and about the resources and tasks given to them. Centuries later, when the prophet Malachi was arguing for greater social and material equality, he went back to these original events and pleaded, 'Don't we all have the same father? Didn't the same God create us all?' (Malachi 2:10).

As implied in the reference to Malachi, the original equality did not last for long. God also created men and women with choice, with the capacity to follow evil as well as good. Consequently, often by violent means, they began to accumulate land, wealth, income, power and position in disproportionate ways, so that some had much while others had little. The outcomes grieved God to the extent that he intervened with words of warning and exhortation and then with laws. In particular, he instituted the Year of Jubilee, as recorded in the books of Leviticus and Deuteronomy, which decreed that periodically debts were cancelled, slaves freed and land returned to its original shareout. As Professor Brian Griffiths puts it, 'The Jubilee laws... were designed to prevent the development of a cycle of permanent deprivation.'[11]

God's valuation of humankind was evident in the Jubilee laws. He wanted all individuals to share in the abundance of society. Yet these laws were largely ignored. Prophets like Hosea, Amos, Micah and Isaiah hit back by proclaiming not just God's concern for those of his creatures who had become paupers and outcasts but also his anger at the powerful and wealthy whose attitudes and practices denied them their due. The same themes were taken up by the author(s) of the Psalms, who declared God's condemnation of those who 'have plenty and are always getting more' (Psalm 73:12). Then, in three beautiful verses, he describes the ideal king as one who

> rescues the poor who call to him,
> and those who are needy and neglected.
> He has pity on the weak and poor;
> he saves the lives of those in need.
> He rescues them from oppression and violence;
> their lives are precious to him.
> *Psalm 72:12–14*

So precious to God are the lives of the oppressed that the coming of the Messiah, the Christ, was linked with concern for them. When Mary met her pregnant relative, Elizabeth, she was filled with the Holy Spirit and gave voice to what was later called the Magnificat. In some of the strongest words in scripture, Mary rejoiced that God

> has brought down mighty kings from their thrones,
> and lifted up the lowly.
> He has filled the hungry with good things,
> and sent the rich away with empty hands.
> *Luke 1:52–53*

Within a few years, Elizabeth's own son, John the Baptist, was preparing the way for Mary's son, Jesus. When eager listeners asked John what they should do, he replied in practical terms, 'Whoever has two shirts must give one to the man who has none, and whoever has food must share it' (Luke 3:11). The Baptist was revealing that the Christ would place great value on the poor.

Jesus was not born into a royal palace but in a stable. His childhood friends were not the sons and daughters of successful financiers and powerful politicians but those of ordinary village dwellers. When he began his ministry, he scandalized the establishment by giving little time to the rich and famous, and instead showed his love for beggars, lepers, prostitutes, the outcasts of society. He did not exclude the top brass, and indeed he sometimes asked them to give their wealth to the poor and to follow him. But his disciples and followers were overwhelmingly made up of ordinary folk, the fishermen, traders, labourers and – unusual for that era – women and foreigners. Jesus was astonishingly radical in that he called and gave responsibility to those who socially and materially were in the bottom percentage of the time. Further, he often told parables which contained warnings for the rich while exalting the poverty-stricken. He summed up his teaching by restating what he called the greatest commandments: 'Love the Lord your God with all your heart, with all your soul, and with all your mind. This is the greatest and the most important commandment. The second most important commandment is like it: Love your neighbour as you love yourself' (Matthew 22:37–40). The implication is that human beings were intended to have a personal, loving, worshipping relationship with God and, as that God has created all humans as equals, so love must exist between them. Indeed, God's creatures are told to love others 'as you love yourself'. There can be little doubt that God values all human beings and that they are expected to love others, including – indeed especially – the poor, the despised, the rejected.

These teachings and practices did not make Jesus popular with the political and religious establishments. He was crucified between two thieves. Yet he rose from the dead and revealed himself, not to academic leaders or mighty landowners but to humble women who had followed him around, to two travellers not rich enough to afford horses, and to the mixture of fishermen, tax collectors, labourers and peasants who made up his disciples. The pattern continued into the early church. The apostle Paul reminded one fellowship, 'From the human point of view few of you were wise or powerful or of high social standing. God purposely chose what the world considers nonsense in order to shame the wise, and he chose what the world considers weak in order to shame the powerful. He chose what the world looks down on and despises, and thinks is nothing, in order to destroy what the world thinks is important' (1 Corinthians 1:26–29).

There can be little doubt that God holds all people to be not only valuable but equally valuable. He counters the worldly bias towards the rich and powerful by displaying a special concern for the well-being of the poor and powerless. If Jesus had been born into Britain in the 1990s, he would not have dwelt in the luxurious suburbs, would not have attended the private schools, would not have worked on the stock exchange. Instead he would probably have been born in the inner city, raised on a council estate, befriended the homeless, made a church from drug abusers, lone parents, low wage earners, the unemployed. He would not have excluded the privileged. On the contrary, he would have tried to reconcile them with the deprived by calling upon them to share their goods and follow him.

Where does this leave those who want to take seriously the Bible's message about greater equality, who want to value people in the way God does, who want to follow in the footsteps of the Jesus who sought the poorest, who want to obey the promptings of the Holy Spirit to be socially and spiritually inclusive and not exclusive? They can take the gospel of reconciliation to all – not just to those in the detached houses in the prosperous south of England. They can campaign for a more equal society and attempt to put principles into practice in their own styles of living. More particularly, and with reference to the theme of this book, they can make an issue of the exclusion of many of the bottom 30 per cent from the vehicles of public communication. They should do so for two reasons.

First, because it is an expression of the value they place upon the poor. They can affirm the biblical message that all people are of equal importance to God by striving to put them on the same footing as others in terms of expressing their views and wishes. To do so is to side with the Psalmist when he wrote, 'The needy will not always be neglected; the hope of the poor will not be crushed for ever' (Psalm 9:18).

Second, because in a small way, the fight for access to

the media is a part of the battle for greater equality. To encourage poor people to publish is to challenge the mechanisms which uphold inequality. A major means by which the top 40 per cent retain their positions and possessions is by their control of words. No serious challenge is made against inequality because the beneficiaries produce the words of newspapers, books, TV, radio and parliament. By contrast, those who identify with those who are not allowed to publish will identify with the Psalmist when he wrote of the wicked, 'Silence those flattering tongues, O Lord! Close those boastful mouths that say, "With our words we get what we want. We will say what we wish, and no one can stop us"' (Psalm 12:3–4). Those at the bottom cannot silence the mighty. But, wherever possible, they should seek to release and propagate the words of those who are most precious to God. Of course, the words and publications will appear feeble, even laughable, to those who hold power. But the words and perceptions of the weak could be one means of undermining the values and assumptions by which the strong justify their ownership of too much of the resources which God intended for others.

## Users strike back

These paragraphs are not intended to imply that those in the bottom 30 per cent are completely docile and make no attempts to express themselves. It is not just in regard to newspaper articles and TV appearances that members of the bottom 30 per cent are kept at bay. Many of them are clients or users of the social services yet they have had little say in how these services are shaped and administered. In recent years, however, some users have challenged the traditional practice that they should be treated simply as grateful recipients. A leading campaigner has been Peter Beresford, himself a former user and member of a mental health project called Survivors Speak Out. Funds were obtained to establish a Citizens' Commission on the Future of the Welfare State. Within it, disabled people, lone parents, carers, recipients of state pensions and other users were able to present their analyses of the strengths and weaknesses of welfare services.[12]

In 1997, Peter Beresford and his colleagues compiled a bibliography of individuals and groups who had produced materials relating to their own social exclusion.[13] It included pieces written by people with learning difficulties, disabled people, mental health service users and elderly people. Significantly, the smallest section, just five references, concerned 'people with experiences of poverty'.

One of the references was to ATD Fourth World, an organization which originated in France under the inspiration of Father Joseph Wresinski. It has used its slender resources to work with 'the poorest of the poor' and is based on the premise that they should be involved at all levels of decision-making. It mounted a research project, *Talk With Us, Not At Us*, which demonstrated that low-income families were able to participate in, speak with and negotiate with social work professionals.[14] ATD Fourth World has also organized policy forums at which members addressed professionals from the social services. Another organization to take seriously the views of poor people is Church Action on Poverty, an ecumenical body, which has promoted Local People: National Voice. The latter has brought together people with experience of poverty to a number of national hearings at which they expressed their opinions on the nature of the welfare state along with an analysis of which policies and programmes would best tackle poverty and inequality. It is encouraging, too, to see researchers, like Roger Green, writing in close co-operation with local residents.[15]

## Poor writing

Despite the above examples and despite the appearance of privately published writings (often poetry) by women's groups, it is still unusual for residents of deprived areas to be allowed to write not just about the social services but also about their own lives, their battles to survive, their neighbourhoods. Consequently, the experiences of members of the excluded 30 per cent, as seen by themselves, are rarely published.

Having worked – and occasionally been unemployed – on two council estates for over twenty years, I became convinced that a number of residents lacked not the ability to write but rather the opportunity to publish. The matter was brought home to me when visiting a woman struggling to bring up four children in a damp flat. She told me that she found great difficulties in talking about her family with social workers. But she added, 'It's not because I don't have feelings, not because I don't think about it. I just clam up.' She then confided to me that, after the children were in bed, she often wrote down what she was thinking and feeling. Knowing that I was a writer, she showed me her work. I took home the scraps of paper, the backs of envelopes, pages torn out of school exercise books, on which she had expressed her thoughts. I was moved not just by the emotions expressed but also by their coherence and reason. She was delighted with my praise and I suggested she bring her pieces together in an article. Initially she laughingly dismissed the suggestion, said she couldn't do it, that she was not a writer, that nobody would be interested in what she wrote. I persisted and, with encouragement, she produced an article. It was published in a social work magazine and the woman was thrilled that she was in print and that she received some much-needed cash.

The experience gave me faith that poor people could write. It combined with my egalitarian belief that such people should have access to publishing their views. I sought funds for a project which I entitled Poor Writing. James Cornford of the Paul Hamlyn Foundation and Ben Whitaker and Paul Curno of the Gulbenkian Foundation were enthusiastic about the idea and facilitated my applications. Subsequently, I was able to spend time in encouraging and paying seven people to write. The time and help I gave varied. One woman required just three visits and produced well-typed drafts. Others needed more frequent help in regard to content and construction and produced handwritten material, sometimes a page at a time. Two completed their task by recording it on tape. I have edited the material and taken out repetition, but the work is their own.

I knew all the contributors because they were residents of the Easterhouse housing scheme in Glasgow, although some have since moved. One I met when visiting the local housing co-operative, two at the Salvation Army, one at the youth clubs which started at the Salvation Army and were later transferred to FARE (Family Action in Rogerfield & Easterhouse). The others I met through FARE, which is a local neighbourhood group; it runs a number of youth clubs, and my first contact with the families was through the attendance of their children. I am well pleased with what they have written; I am convinced that they do bring a different slant from the writers from outside. Their contributions now follow.

*Notes*
1.  CES, *Outer Estates in Britain: Easterhouse Case Study*, Centre for Environmental Studies, 1985, pp. 1, 5.
2.  C. Murray, *The Emerging British Underclass*, Institute of Economic Affairs, 1990, pp. 12, 21.
3.  A. Massie, column in the *Glasgow Herald*, 13 November 1988.
4.  D. Harrison, 'Why Glaswegians prefer to slum it', *The Observer*, 31 October 1993.
5.  M. Pacione, *Glasgow*, Wiley, 1995, pp. 225, 234.
6.  B. Holman, 'Shaken not stirred', *The Guardian*, 22 January 1994.
7.  Cited by R. Pigott, 'The executive exodus', *The Guardian*, 24 September 1997.
8.  W. Hutton, *The State We're In*, Jonathan Cape, 1995, ch. 1.
9.  B. Holman, *Towards Equality: A Christian Manifesto*, SPCK, 1997, p. 26.
10. R. Tawney, *The Attack and Other Papers*, Allen & Unwin, 1981, pp. 182–83.
11. D. Anderson (ed.), *The Kindness That Kills*, SPCK, 1984, p. 109.

12. P. Beresford and M. Turner, *It's Our Welfare: Report of the Citizens' Commission on the Welfare State*, National Institute of Social Work, 1996.
13. P. Beresford, K. Stalker and A. Wilson, *Speaking for Ourselves*, Social Work Research Centre, University of Stirling, 1997.
14. ATD Fourth World, *Talk With Us, Not At Us*, Fourth World Publications, 1996.
15. R. Green, *Community Action Against Poverty*, Kingsmead Kabin, 1997.

# Part 2

# The Right Writers

## Carol

I was born in the hospital in Paisley. My parents were moving to Easterhouse and my brother and sister were already there. My start in life was not too good as I had one leg shorter than the other so I had to have a pin put in my leg and I was in Ruchill Hospital for a year. I was even on TV when the cameras came to the hospital. I was plastered up to my chest and had an iron bar across my chest but I was still crawling across the floor. As far as I know, my mother did come up every day but perhaps the bond between us did not develop. I came home but had to go every year for an X-ray until I was 14. The pin was taken out and I have a massive scar on my hip which I am paranoid about. But it was one thing which was successful in my life because I did walk OK.

We moved to Easterhouse in 1960. It was before Commonhead, where I later lived, was even built.

Canonbie Street was the bus terminus and I can remember the 41 and the 211 were the buses to town, the 22 went to Castlemilk and the 230 to Parkhead. Down in Lochdochart Road, where the new shops are now, there was Frank Boyle's the butcher, a co-op shop, a newspaper shop and a chemist's.

My brother and sister were quite a bit older than me. By the time I was ten, my brother was married. I remember my sister had a boyfriend, she was engaged. We had a two-bedroomed flat so I shared with her. I used to hide under the blanket when my sister came in and kissed him. She was eight years older than me and she used to say, 'You were just a mistake. You shouldn't have been born.' That hurt me. I put on a front, the 'I don't care' personality, but I really did.

Our dad was a real father figure. He worked all hours and our mum would say, 'Wait till your father gets home,' and then he would give us a chastisement. He went out to work before I got up for school and when he came in at supper time my brother, sister and myself would sometimes run out in case we had been in trouble. If my dad walked into the living room, you got up from his chair. My dad was a working man, a good worker, but he was not one for sitting with you.

I got on all right with my mum, she was my 'mammy' and I put her on a pedestal. She was bad with her nerves and she was never one to cuddle me. It was not the lovable relationship that I wanted. I am now an insecure person and I think it goes back to my childhood. My mum took a breakdown when I was eight. I remember on my eighth birthday going to Gartloch Hospital and having a party on the ward with the nurses. The breakdown was caused by neighbours downstairs who were partygoers. They would drink and fight until all hours of the morning. My mum was in hospital for quite a long time and my granny looked after us. I became more attached to her than my mother.

My dad was an engineer at a firm which built cranes. One day he did not come home. He had had a bad accident. Someone dropped his cigarette when he was driving a fork-lift truck and put it into the wrong gear and pinned my father to the wall. He stopped breathing a couple of times in the ambulance but he lived. His brother, my uncle, went with him to the hospital and there was a delay in telling my mum (who was now home). She resented this and they had a lot of ill-feeling. My dad eventually got back to work but could not do the same as before. He became an odd-job guy. He was always very good with money. He had a purse and he put away a ten bob note each week which he saved to buy my mum a birthday and Christmas present. He always said that he never wanted for anything because he never needed anything. Every Friday he came home and his pay packet had not been opened. They used to slag him at work for that.

I went to Bishoploch Primary School. It was a big school then and had a top, middle and back part. I used to get into trouble but it was harmless trouble. I used to disrupt the class but it was not like today when children throw chairs about and abuse the teachers. I would start laughing until I got put outside – with my desk. I got on great with the headmaster, Mr Johnston. Every Tuesday and Thursday the minister would come and do a service.

I got up at seven o'clock and went to school, and the janitor, Mr Watson, let me put all the chairs out in the dining room for the service. I never achieved anything in the classroom but I was always doing something. I did country dancing. I loved sport and ran for the school. I had so much energy.

I went to Lochend Secondary School. We once went on strike so that the lassies could wear trousers. We walked off school on the pitches and the TV came. We won. When I look back I can see that I was like my daughter is now. I got into every bit of trouble that was going. I would get caught making faces when others did not. I did things for a laugh just to get attention. Hardly a day went by when I did not get the belt. But the teachers liked me. One teacher used to take me outside and hit the belt on the landing instead of on me. I was old for my age and I started going out with an older boy, he was 17. Again I think it was for attention. It ended with me being sexually assaulted, raped.

Then we moved to Cranhill. I remember the day we moved all the furniture out of the house and I was still in it. It broke my heart. Easterhouse was my roots. I changed schools but I could not settle in. Every day I was coming back to Easterhouse. After a couple of years we came back to Easterhouse. I was about 15 and I never went back to school. I got a Saturday job in Healey's the grocers in Queen Street in Glasgow. I was serving and I was good with the public. But because I was with older people I got into smoking and drinking. During the week I just used to hang about. There wasn't much to do. The Easterhouse Project was in the steel huts with roller-skating on Saturday nights and football for boys. That was the only thing.

I ended up getting a job full time down at the Clyde doing sewing in a factory. Not long after that I got married. I was always insecure so I married the first bloke I really went out with. I met Fred in the gangs I used to hang about with. I never really loved him. I was only 17 and he was two years older. That made a difference. I needed a male figure. I had a row about it with my mum and dad who did not want me to get married, so I moved in with his parents in Cranhill. I thought I was so smart but it broke my heart to be away from them. Fred's dad was blind and I got on great with him. We got married in the registry office. My mum and dad came to the wedding. I know my mum was hurting inside, she was still my mammy.

So we got married and moved to Springboig. I got a job in an ice cream factory at Toll Cross. But I had no life. I should have known what kind of person he was. I never got on with him but he was obsessed with me. I hated it and my mum knew I hated it. He battered me stupid and after two years I moved into a hostel. He knew where I worked and he waited for me one day and pulled me into a post. I was admitted to the Royal Infirmary. He had gone home and slashed his wrists so I was in one ward and he was in another. My mum came in, took one look at me and said, 'Enough's enough.'

I ended up getting my own flat back in Glassel Road, Easterhouse. I moved in and slept on the bare floorboards for I had nothing. I have always been able to manage money, I have never been stupid with it, and gradually I got a home together. While I was staying at the hostel I had got friendly with a girl who became my sister-in-law. It was the worst thing that ever happened to me. She came from a very insecure background and she was a thief. She did not steal from people but from shops. I had a night job in a pub in Sauchiehall Street and she used to come in to see me. My brother Archie – who was on the rebound from his first wife – also came in and they met. So the two moved in with me until they got their own place and they had two girls – my nieces.

I had another pal who moved in with me, another one from an insecure background, it was as though I was mothering them. One night I went dancing with her and met my second man, Ernie. He was a nice looking guy but looks are not everything as I have found out the hard way. We got married at the registry office and he moved in. I must have it written on my face 'batter me' because that is what he did. He worked and I worked. I reckon this is why it lasted so long. I was only eighteen and a half and I don't think I realized the meaning of the wedding vows. Yet I did not like the idea of living with somebody, I did not think that was right. I got married for the security, not for the right reasons. I thought I loved him but I did not know the meaning of love. By this time I was working as a waitress and he was jealous of me. I had to walk along with my head down in case he thought I was looking at somebody. My family stepped in. Also he was fighting some guys in our area and he had to move out. I realized I did not need him and I got divorced. I wanted more, I wanted to be loved and cuddled, what I had missed as a child.

Then I met the man who was to be Miranda's dad. I had got to the stage when I did not like going out so I got a CB and I met Jack through that. I was nearly 21 when Miranda was conceived. But he did not move in with me. I had had enough. It would make me feel as though I was living in sin. He would stay a couple of nights a week and that was all. He was only 17 and very immature. Once Miranda was born there was no input from him. He would not even carry her. But his mum and my mum were a great help.

I was in hospital for a lot of the pregnancy. I was on tranquillizers, tablets for epilepsy and asthma. There was talk of a termination. Even before Miranda was born, I felt that decisions were being made about us. In the hospital, in the wooden huts on Duke Street, I met Dr Hunt, who became a part of my life. Once Miranda was born I stayed in the hospital for three weeks and later I went back in again. Because of my social circumstances and because of all the medication, I was put under the social worker in the hospital. I felt I never had the chance to be alone with my baby. I felt that decisions were being made above me because I was a single parent. It was hard for me to say no to officials, because in the eyes of the Social Work Department (SWD) that is you rejecting help and then they take you to the panels. When I left hospital, the hospital social worker contacted Easterhouse and one came round. I resented that. I was told I would get a homemaker, but I did not need one because I can manage a house fine. But because I was a single parent and living on benefit you had to go along with having your baby supervised. Often I felt I was only mother in name. I had parental rights but I always felt they could be removed. In a sense I felt I had already lost Miranda because it was implied that I could not bring her up myself.

While Miranda was still a baby, social work got her to a nursery every day. I had to go as well. They wanted to see how I acted with her. I had a nice flat, I did not starve her, they could not get me for neglect, so they made me attend to watch me. There is nothing worse than somebody else telling you what to do with your baby. You are constantly under their supervision. I had to go there. I could not relax. It was not a placement for Miranda to learn, it was a placement for me. They never saw me at home. I was still on tablets. They never provided the kind of day care which gave me a break. They never helped me get a fire guard. Did not see if I was cooking properly.

I did not realize that I had a say in the matter. I took it for granted that because I was a single parent I had to do what they wanted. They never told me my rights. I had umpteen social workers. They did not help me to cope, they just decided they would remove Miranda. I just wanted someone to talk to. By this time my mum had died. My dad had bought his own house with some money that had been left him, but he was a prisoner in it, hardly ever went out. But he did take us to places in the car – but he wasn't the same as my mammy. I wanted someone to listen to me and not make judgments. I was nervous and I kept the house too tidy. Miranda did not have much of a life because I hardly let her play with anything because I did not like a mess. This was because of my nerves.

I was on my own with Miranda. I had relationships on and off, but they never lasted because if they did not like my Miranda that was just tough. My child always came first. I really cared for her. I knew I lacked what they called 'consistency' in the way I treated her, but nobody ever told me what that long word meant. Then I discovered that I let her do one thing one minute and another the next. But it was hard being a single parent. I just knew that if she fell you gave her a cuddle. She was the mirror image of me and that was not her fault.

Archie, my brother, broke up with his partner and moved in with me with his two children. So I had three children under five, all in nappies. The SWD gave me permission to look after the three. My brother had nothing, his flat had been boarded up. The SWD did not help us, did not even give us single beds. Archie stayed two years. He was working and had to get up at six in the morning. I was the one who got up in the night when the children were sick. So from somebody who was supposed not to be coping with one child, I went to looking after three. I used to take Miranda up to the nursery, Juliet to another nursery and Babs with a child-minder and then back to the nursery.

Archie later moved to Denmilne Street. Miranda was now four or five. I moved to Commonhead where I had my own back and front door. I had to pay a backhander to get it. It was the worst move I ever made, I never settled there. When Archie moved, I went along to the Salvation Army to get some secondhand furniture for him. It was there I met Captain Buchanan. I could hardly believe him. In his old, baggy pullover, if it wasn't for his

Salvation Army cap you would have thought he had come in looking for somewhere to stay. He was always rushing around for people. He was a bit like myself, he thought for others not for himself.

I started going to the services on a Sunday. The SWD was getting really heavy with me and I was looking for something else to turn to apart from my dad. I was so mixed up and I wanted to test myself. 'Do I believe or not believe?' and if I did believe I wanted to know why all these things were happening to me. I got my daughter christened at the Sally. I started helping the captain at a Tuesday lunch club which he started for men, mostly alcoholics. I enjoyed that. When I saw the look on some of the guys' faces when I gave them mince and tatties, it made me realize how lucky I was. Never once did any of them say anything bad to me or try anything. I was able to help one man. He was Old Jonah the Brickie who lived near me. I took a lot of stick from the men over him, I think he told them I was his girlfriend. I tried to get him off the drink. I used to let him come in the house. He was company for me because you need a relationship. It was friendship. I went up to his wife's house, they were separated, on a Sunday and got dinner. Jonah saw what I was like whereas others saw me as this cheeky, arrogant person whose defences were always up against the whole world. He saw me as a human being which is something the SWD never did.

I enjoyed the services at the Sally and looked forward to them. I met friends there like the Thomsons and people who never held ill feelings against you. They always wanted to help, they gave me time and explained things. The SWD had taken away all my confidence. At times I could not talk, I would just break down. I started to believe in God for selfish reasons at first. He was the only one who I could talk to and did not say bad things to me. God listened and gave me strength.

I first saw Phil when he was with Bob Holman in his Morris Minor. Bob stopped to speak to me and I thought, 'I wonder who he is?' Then we met at the Sally. Phil never moved in with me. He had a daughter, Wilma, and they would come down to me and we would go up to his place. We were more pals than anything and I was like a mother to Wilma. Phil expected too much of his daughter. Emotional things were happening to her and he never really understood them. She would wet herself a bit, the things you could not tell a man. Phil was involved with the SWD as well. Because the SWD ruled me, I told my social worker about him. Then his social worker came round to see me. Then she told him how bad I was and that he could end up losing Wilma. The same with my social worker who said, 'Phil is bad news, you'll end up losing Miranda.' We were both told not to see each other. So they split us up. I think we could have helped each other. But I did not know my rights.

After that I got very low, depressed. I told my social worker how bad I was feeling. She went back to the SWD and then I had a phone call from them to say if I did not find a place somewhere else for Miranda within eight hours they would come and lift her. They may have acted because I had had a blow-up with Miranda and because they thought I was still seeing Phil. I was desperate. My dad was away. I phoned up Bob who lived nearby. Bob had a reputation for getting people their rights, and I knew the social work was not happy with that. But I had nothing to lose. He went and asked Miranda's granny if she could take her, which she did. I then went into psychiatric hospital. While I was there, I was told that Miranda would be going into temporary foster care. When I came out, I learnt that the SWD had taken out a place of safety order on Miranda but left her with the grannie. I went into a panic and got in touch with Bob. His advice was that I needed to be properly represented and he phoned around and then got a lawyer who was good on childcare matters. So we went to court and the judge said that the SWD had not got sufficient grounds. So Miranda came home again. She and I never had a mother–daughter relationship because the bond was never there. It was taken away even when she was in the womb and people were telling me what to do with her even before she was born. This taking her away only made it worse.

The SWD then started to work closely with Miranda's school. If the school had any complaints, if Miranda was in a bad mood, the social worker was soon at my door asking, 'Why was she in a bad mood?' They never gave us a chance and I ended up going back into hospital. My dad took Miranda but he was suffering from gout and the social workers told him he was not fit enough to look after her. Then dad went into hospital and the social workers put Miranda into a temporary foster home saying it was until he came out. But by this time closed adoption was on the agenda. Miranda did not get on well with the foster parents, they never listened to her. She was moved to another foster home. By this time I had come home but I was still mixed up, still insecure, but I received no help for that. At the beginning I was allowed to see Miranda quite a lot. She got upset and this was used against me. Instead of saying, 'Miranda is upset because she is missing her mum,' they said 'When Miranda gets upset, the foster parents can't cope with her.' They then started supervising the visits.

I had moved from Commonhead to Lochdochart Road. I started doing voluntary work with Helping Hands in Carntyne. You got £10 on top of your broo[1] money. You sat with old people and gave them company and time. It was good for me. Everyone around me seemed angry with me, blaming me for the split-up with Miranda. I was glad to visit lonely people who were not angry. It was while doing this that I met Justin, who was also a volunteer.

The social workers said that they could not fault me on the home front, on the food I prepared. My downfall was being a single parent, and they said I lacked consistency. I was up and down because of the different tablets the doctors were prescribing me. These gave me mood swings, and sometimes these had not agreed with Miranda. She was the opposite of me. If I was high, she would be down.

The social workers told me that they were going to go for permanent fostering for Miranda. Then I fell pregnant and lost the baby. I was feeling ill and vulnerable and at this point the SWD told me Miranda would be placed for adoption. I remember it because it was Miranda's eighth birthday and I had been allowed to have a party for her.

The social worker was there and turned to me and said, 'Enjoy it because it's your last.' I was determined to fight this. My dad offered to take Miranda again, but it was not allowed. One day the social worker took us all out to the loch, Justin came as well, and she told me to bring photos of Miranda because they were making her a Life Story Book so that she would be able to look back at the years she had had with me. I was told that closed adoption meant it was closed to the family so that anyone who had known her would not be able to see her again. The daft thing was that sometimes Miranda would run away from the foster home and phone me. Miranda was told that she would not be able to go home again, and they gave her the impression that I did not want her as I was having another baby. It was horrendous.

I got the solicitor again. She was good and I was able to explain to her what was happening. We went to a Children's Hearing where she spoke for me as a friend because she could not represent me as a lawyer there. Miranda had said she wanted to be with me. The panel criticized the social workers for the way they had handled matters.

By this time Justin and I had got married. I got pregnant again and was in hospital resting prior to having wee Justin. The social worker phoned the doctor, who told me I would get a phone call later and that it was positive. The call then told me to come to the social work office when I came out of hospital. The news was that they wanted to rehabilitate Miranda. It harmed her. She had been led to believe that she was never coming back because her mother could not cope with her. They never told her about the parts of me that can cope. Miranda was back within a fortnight, but she was given no explanation as to why. I am still not sure why the social workers changed their minds. They said they took her because they were concerned about Miranda, but in that case, shouldn't they have been concerned about the baby I was carrying. If I was a danger to children why did they do nothing about that. I know they left a mess behind them. They split the family up. Many people were made to think that I was not much of a mother.

Miranda was away for over a year and it was hell. I would look out of the back window at the Campsies and tears would stream down my eyes. It was because she was not there and I had the thought of not having her again. But it was difficult for Miranda when she came back. I had got married, a new man and a new baby on the way. She got flung in the deep end. Gradually she settled, although there was no help from the SWD. Justin was great. I have lived a lot of my life in the past. I am still insecure. Social work has made me live in the past by always looking at how I used to treat Miranda. Justin has made me live in the present. He threw all my tablets away. I called him everything because I did not think I could survive without them. It was like flinging my life down the toilet pan. But now I am off them completely. From the beginning Justin made it clear that Miranda would never come between us. It was hard for him because he had to get to like her and to build up his defence mechanisms. It was also hard for me. I was a wife and mother and had to give them both a lot of attention. Also Miranda's real dad lived just up the road.

Miranda came back in 1991. Justin was born soon after and is now six. Now we also have Alan, who is three, and Lucy, who is just over three months. Miranda is frightened to show her feelings because I think she is still afraid that she may have to go away again. The SWD closed the case on her, but then, last year, she was sexually assaulted. Three boys were involved. It was horrible. She did not wash for two days. She had to go to Yorkhill Hospital where they even took scrapings from her teeth, particles from her hair, and took away her clothes. At least she got some counselling. I found it difficult to support her as it brought back all that happened to me. Justin was there. He got up at night when she had nightmares. She put Justin through hell because he is a male figure, but I suppose at least she was secure enough to take it out on him. The boys denied the charge at the Children's Hearing so it was sent to court for proof. Miranda had to go as a witness. We were there for two days. When she went in she had to be in the same room as the idiot that did it. It was found proven and he went away to a place for young offenders. But now he is out and walks up and down the streets. One night he got on the same bus as Miranda so she jumped off although she had no more money and had to walk.

My family is more happy now. But I am still insecure, not because of Justin and the kids but because of my upbringing and things I can't get answers to because my mum and dad are not here any more. I went into the SWD and went back over my records. There were things in them which I did not like and things with which I disagreed. Again, I realize that the social workers never told me my rights, never informed me about the law and where I could have got help.

I am determined that Miranda will not go back into care. She is like me. Her defences are always up, she thinks everybody dislikes her and she is not very positive. We rely upon Justin. I survive but Justin is my life. I still don't think I could stand on my own feet. I still get panic attacks. He supports me 100 per cent. Justin is a houseman, he loves his kids, he loves being with them, spending time with them. He doesn't go to the pub, he doesn't bet. I get disability living allowance, so we manage financially.

Over the years it has helped me to help others. I like helping people. While Miranda was away I got involved with a food co-op. Bob asked Justin to help out with the driving and then I went along. I did the till, I went in the van or our car to buy the food in the morning from cheap supermarkets and cash-and-carrys. In the beginning, they did not know we were from a co-op and thought we were buying all the cheap food to sell at a profit in a shop. Once I went in to the back to explain to the manager who we were, and when I opened the door to his office he and a woman were snogging away. I think he was so embarrassed that he agreed to us having large quantities. Later I was elected chairperson. It gave me a purpose. The volunteers were mainly elderly people, so some were like mother figures or granny figures to me. They respected me and it gave me more confidence.

You could get your basic stuff at the co-op. People without much money could call on a Monday and get enough to last them all week. Having a young family, I knew what mothers wanted like beans, sausage and beans, ravioli, soup, jam, and all at prices much cheaper than the shops across the road. In fact some of the shop owners were not very nice to us because we were taking business from them. Mothers with three or four children and old people have not got cars or can't travel to the big shops by bus. They go to the local shops or to the vans whose prices are extortionate. They charged 50p for a loaf whereas the co-op sold at 20–25p.

Our food co-op was voluntary and it needed a lot of input from people, really needed a full-time coordinator. Given training for the helpers and commitment, co-ops can survive, and we did for a couple of years. Unfortunately, the place was isolated from our community, it was in the wing of a school. Break-ins started. You could see young people coming in and eyeing us up and down. I had to run helpers home if they were carrying money. Some thieves hid up the stairs until we had gone and then smashed the place up and took the goods. It got to the stage where we were frightened to go in in the morning in case of what had happened. We had to close and that was a shame.

I am now a part of the Easterhouse Breast Feeding Initiative. Only 6 per cent of mothers breast feed in Easterhouse, the lowest figure in Britain. So some money was put into this project by the Greater Glasgow Health Board, and it is run by mothers who have breast fed. We get names of women who book into maternity at Rotten Row Hospital and then we visit them. It is voluntary although we get any expenses. Breast feeding is good for babies. Bottle feeding is less hygienic, you can never get rid of all the germs. You don't have to scrub your breasts

– although some women think you do! The body has oils which keep the skin OK. Breast feeding cuts down sickness and diarrhoea. The milk is at the right consistency and temperature and is easier for babies to digest. Breast feeding is natural and convenient. However, we do not force mothers into it. We do not put pressure on them and make them feel guilty. The aim is to educate them so that mothers have the option of breast feeding. A lot of people don't consider breast feeding. Some are even embarrassed to talk about breasts because of all the sexual thing about boobs. Some are influenced by grannies who did not breast feed. At one door, the granny answered and said, 'She doesn't want to breast feed' and shut the door in my face. We educate and support mothers. If they do start we can help them through difficulties. I can identify with them because I had problems with breast feeding. I do get hurt sometimes when I think someone is going to start and they don't. We survive because we've got a lot of humour in the team. And we became well known with people stopping us in the street when they recognized us.

The research has now been completed and the figures collected. We can say that attitudes have changed and I think more mothers are trying it. We won a prize when the Greater Glasgow Health Board presented us with a Certificate of Merit.

I am a different person now from ten years ago. I look at things in their wholeness now instead of jumping in. I used to be constantly negative, now I am more positive. It is because I met people who supported me. I have been helped by going to the Sally, by being a part of the food co-op, by the Breast Feeding Initiative. These are positive things. I've been supported and now I can support others. But I could have done none of these without Justin. It was Justin who persuaded me to breast feed because he knew it was better for the kids. I wish that I had breast fed Miranda then she would have weighed more. But you love them all the same.

Miranda is now a teenager. Easterhouse is not an easy place for teenagers. The days of tapping on a door and running away are over, youngsters want more than that. It is not just Easterhouse. There is a lot of hatred and violence in the world today. But there are not many amenities for them in Easterhouse. FARE has clubs up in its bit but there is not much down the bottom end. The sports centre is quite expensive and it is in the centre where a lot of kids will not go in case they get jumped. Sports centres and community centres need to be in each area so that they are for each community.

I have stayed here all my days. I have seen people grow up and leave. Years ago you tapped somebody's door and they asked you in for a wee cup of tea. Now some are frightened to open the door. Drugs is a problem. The sad thing is that many druggies turn to stealing to pay for it. Drugs destroy a community because people can be a pal to you one day and an enemy the next. You can get up and be as cheerful as anything and then you get kicked up and down the street. Just last weekend there was a murder, a nineteen-year-old boy. He'd been to a party and was just a couple of hundred yards from his own house. I know his dad and he must be feeling terrible because he has already split up from his wife.

There are needle exchanges which are good but not enough. More counselling services are required. Kids need to be educated to show them the dangers of drugs. But it is not just enough to say 'Easterhouse is a deprived area' unless something gets done. I hope the new government will make a difference. They want better education and that's right but you can get every certificate in the book and when you go for a job they say, 'Where do you stay, G33, G34? We'll let you know.' There are no jobs here. And if a company does come in and puts up, say, a garage, it will have its own staff brought in, it will not be staffed by people from Easterhouse. The government should put money into Easterhouse because others won't. And the jobs should be for local people. But we must act as well. Easterhouse has a bad reputation for drugs, violence, deprivation. People should be able to walk through their own scheme instead of getting stabbed. We must act because the community needs to be for each other.

# Bill

I was born in Carntyne, Glasgow. We moved to Castlemilk. I have a lot of memories about my dad. He was tough but he was good with us. In his eyes we always came first. For some reason we had to move from Castlemilk. I am not sure why. My dad did not want to move back to Carntyne in case he got back to drinking there again. So we had to move to Easterhouse, to Dalilea Drive. I was about eight and I was quite scared at first, scared of a new school and I felt I would not make pals. Dad took us to St Clare's School and I started to make pals. A couple of weeks after that my dad died. That hurt my mum and us children really bad. I did not really understand what had happened for a while. We went into care for a couple of weeks and when I came back I brought some presents for my big brother, mum and dad. I asked mum where dad was but she was in shock and could not tell me and just said he was out. I went to the van and one of my sister's pals said, 'Your dad's dead.' I just ran into the house and would not come out of my room.

When I was about ten, I met Bob, the club leader. Andrew, who was our neighbour, took me to the Sally where Bob was playing games with everyone. I joined a boys club called Covenanters where we had tournaments and you got a trophy. I have still got those trophies I won and I keep them beside my bed and when I look at them I think of those happy days. I wish those days were back for they were the best I had. I liked the club nights, but most of all I liked going to camp in the summer at West Runton in England. I went four or five times. I loved just arriving there, it was great to see the tents again. It was brilliant, just like being in a foreign country. I liked seeing all your friends again which you had made the year before. I liked everything about camp, the quiet time in the morning, the talks, going out. I made some great friends with some of the leaders, Richard and Ruth, Dave, Laurie. They were good people. Richard was my first tent officer, and later my sister and I went to stay for a few days with him and his wife, Ruth. Bob introduced me to his friend Dave. He gave the talks at camp and we all had a good laugh. He was a very funny man. If someone had a bad day, by the time Dave had spoken to them they had forgotten all about it. He was a smashing guy. He lived in Bath and later he and his wife had some of us there for a few days. They made us very welcome. He and his wife took us out all the time, we were never bored, Dave's sister ran a youth club there and she let us go to it. There was a big trampoline there and I was hardly ever off it. The pool table was for free.

Laurie was very easy to talk to. He taught me how to juggle and then to play table tennis, and he always made you feel good at it. Covenanters won a seven-a-side football tournament in Scotland and we went to the finals in London. Laurie got us a place to stay in a church hall. I remember it like yesterday, we stayed up to about eleven playing table tennis. Then we went to the football. I still write to Laurie and he writes back. They were magic days.

By this time I had gone up to secondary school, St Leonard's. I was the joker of the class, always getting into trouble. I could not get on with any of the teachers. I was always getting punishment exercises and suspended. I started dodging school. At the beginning of the third year I was excluded altogether. It was another year before I got into another school, St Andrews. That did not last either, about three months. I had a social worker and he got me into a day assessment centre and I never went back to school.

When I was fifteen or sixteen, I went on a job training scheme doing community industry and then catering. That was a year and a half ago and I have been on the broo since then. I have been trying to get jobs but they keep on saying there are no vacancies or will get in touch but I never hear. I get £57 a fortnight of which I give mum £20. So I get about £18 a week. You can't do much with that.

I am used to living in Easterhouse, but the place has gone downhill. There are too many drugs about. I tried marijuana once. I got talked into it because a few of my pals were smoking. I was sick for ages. They used to laugh at me because I stopped, but not any more. They respect that I don't want to take drugs. I get bored. I get up at about eleven o'clock and I go downstairs and see my mum, have a cup of tea and make some breakfast. Then I go and see if any of my pals are out on the street. If not I just sit and watch the telly. In the evening I might go out and play football. I used to go to the raves at the Tenants

Hall, but there was a lot of fighting and I stopped going. I get depressed sometimes and think about my dad and what it would be like if he were here.

One day I was sitting in my room listening to some music. The door went and my mum shouted up that it was Bob. He asked me if I would like to go the sports centre with him and his son David. It was about time I had a good game of table tennis, I had not played for four or five months. I was a bit stiff at first and David beat me, but then I warmed up and beat Bob.

The very next day, my mum asked me and Paul to go into Glasgow to get some messages (shopping) for her. We got the bus and got off at Glasgow Cross. My brother went into Capital to get the shopping and I waited outside. I had just got my money and I took it out of my pocket to count. Then three guys walked straight up to me and asked me where I was from and pushed me up against the wall. I pushed them back thinking my brother would see what was going on and come out. But he did not. Someone punched me and then I started fighting with them and one said 'Give us your money or you're getting it.' I tried to keep it in my pocket but one took it. By that time someone had called the police and the three guys that robbed me got away with my money. Just then my brother came out of the shop and started chasing after them, shouting at them. After that the police had the cheek to arrest us for breach of the peace. I was the one that got robbed and assaulted and we were the ones that got arrested.

The police got a van to take us to the police station. The way people look at you when you are arrested, they look at you as though you are scum. It made me feel I was dirt and I am not even a criminal. We tried to explain to the police what had happened but they just never listened. They treated me like a criminal and that made it all the more depressing for me. I was hoping I would just wake up out of a bad dream. It is just not fair, if you can't rely on the police to help you, who can you rely upon?

Then walking into a cell like a criminal and getting locked up. It was the first time I had been in a cell, it is terrible. It is just not right and I was so depressed. I was kept in for three nights. It was torture. All you could do was read the names of the people who had been in the cell before and speak to the turnkey – that's the person who brought your food. You only got food every seven hours, at five in the morning, twelve in the afternoon, and seven at night. All you could do was sit and think about your family and friends. It just about brought tears to my eyes just thinking of them and knowing that I was behind a big steel door and could not do anything about it. All I could do was shout to the next cell and talk to my brother. We went for a wash at the same time in the morning but we could only say a couple of words before we were back in our cells. I just wanted to see outside. I wanted to go to court just to get out of the cell.

We got up at 7 a.m. and went in a big bus with lots of other people and went to the Sheriff Court. When we got there we got put in a cell with six other men until three o'clock in the afternoon when we went up to court. I got bail and I should not even have been there in the first place. My brother got kept in till the next day. Just seeing his face when I was walking away from him was horrible,

I felt it was all my fault. But just to see the outside again was magic. I am still waiting to go back to court.

I am too old to go to the camp now, but Bob says that next year I can go as a helper. But last summer he arranged for me to go to Teen Ranch with some others. It is a holiday place near Dundee. There was always something to do. You got up in the morning and had breakfast, had a talk, went to the shop. Then you did an activity, horse-riding, shooting, canoeing, biking. The days were always full and you never got bored. You made a lot of new friends. I liked the talks. It is Christian. Christianity makes me a bit stronger. My mum has always told me to say my prayers before I go to bed.

In the future, I would like to see my mum more happy and my brothers and sisters. I'd like to settle down and get a good job and a good place to live. I want to be able to make sure that my mum is well.

# Erica

I was born in Glasgow but I have little memory of my early days. I know that my dad was cruel to my mum and I have no idea what happened to him. There were four children and myself. We were always in need of money and I hated going to school because I did not have the things that other kids had. When I was about eight, my step-dad appeared.

We moved to Garthamlock, Easterhouse. The council told mum she had to take the house because it was the only one on offer and she took it because all her life she had lived in bedsits and it was her first proper house. Things were OK at first. We lived with our stepdad and he was fine to live with at first, but then things started to happen. He would touch me in places I didn't like. I was scared of him but I knew it was wrong. It didn't happen too often at first but then it became a lot. If I was standing doing the washing-up he would come into the kitchen and put his hand between my legs, I would ask him to stop but he would just go ahead and do it.

I wanted to tell my mum but I was scared it would kill her because she was very poorly at the time. She was waiting to go into hospital for an operation. She was 18–20 stone and she was told she only had a 50–50 chance of surviving it. When she went into hospital things got worse at home with my stepdad. He would make me get into his bed with him and I would cry myself to sleep at night after saying a prayer to God to bring my mum home safe. Then the worst thing happened, mum died and left me all alone in the world. I don't know what was happening to my brother and sisters at the time. My aunt lived in Easterhouse but I never saw much of her after mum died. She was my mum's sister.

I was now eleven or twelve and my body was growing and I was becoming a woman in my eyes. I didn't know what was going on and I had no one to talk to. We lived across the road from the Little Sisters of Mercy. So I used to go to them just to talk and we prayed a lot. I wanted to tell them what was going on at home but I couldn't bring myself to speak about it. At the same time I couldn't cope at school, so I started to play truant or I would be bad and get excluded. Then I started to run away from home, but my stepdad would come into town with his friend from the next close to us and they would look for me, and when they found me he would take me home and things would be the same again. The last time I ran away I was in a shop and I stole something and got caught, so when the police came I told them a false name and I had nowhere to live because both my mum and dad were dead. So they took me to an assessment centre called Beechwood and I hated it. So the first chance I had I ran away with another girl called Bet. We became good friends.

For a long time I kept running away from different homes. In the meantime I tried to sniff glue, I tried all sorts of things and I started to drink in pubs and clubs. I was only thirteen but I passed for older because I was a big girl. I started to hang about with a lot of gay people and drink in gay bars. One day I walked into a gay bar and my brother was sitting there. It was a shock for both of us. Then he asked me if I was gay but I told him no, which was true. He told me he was and I told him, 'So what?'

When I was about fourteen, I met a girl, a bit older than myself, and we got talking. She told me she was working on the streets. I told her I didn't understand, so she said she would show me. She took me up a couple of streets and then we came to a stop at a corner and we just stood there. All these cars were going by, nodding their heads at us. One of the cars stopped and she walked over to it and opened the door. She was talking to the driver for some time. Then she shut the door and walked over to me and told me he wanted me. I asked what she meant by that and she said if I gave him sex he would give me £20. It was tempting but I said no, so she told him. Then she came back and said he would give me £40. I wanted to do it but the sex thing scared me to death. I told her and she told him. They called me over to the car and he said he would give me £50 and he would be kind to me. I asked him to come back in five minutes so I could think it over and he said OK and went away. My friend said I would be daft if I didn't do it. It was hard but it was the idea of all that money plus I had nowhere to go and nowhere to sleep for the night. So when he came back I went with him. He took me to a hotel. When we got to the room I was so scared I went to the bathroom. When I came out he was sitting on the edge of the bed. He asked me if I wanted to forget it. I was tempted to say yes but I needed the money. So I put the lights out and took my clothes off and got into bed with him. I shut my eyes and let him do what he wanted to do. I was glad the light was out so he could not see the silent tears on my face and I prayed it would be over soon and it was. He got up and he dressed in silence while I lay in the bed crying to myself. He sat on the edge of the bed and gave me my £50 plus he said I could sleep in the hotel for the night because it was paid for. Then he went away and I stayed in the bed for what seemed a lifetime. Then I got up and ran a bath and sat in the bath tub for about an hour. I went to bed and lay thinking about mum, dad, my brother and sisters and what I just did with a strange man. But then I thought about the £50 under my pillow so I put it all to the back of my mind. It was hard but I did it.

From then on I worked the streets. I got caught and taken back to different homes. I ran away and met this boy and fell in love with him. I thought he loved me but he just wanted me to work the streets for him, and he told me if I didn't do it he would kill me. So I did it for him, but I felt I was back to square one again with no money in my pocket. The next car I got into I told the man to drop me off somewhere else and he did. So I was on my own again, but by then I was a bit more mature. I was caught again and taken to an assessment centre. I decided to stay for a bit of a rest and that is when I found out I was having a baby. I was only fourteen, so they decided to send me to a mother-and-baby home run by nuns. It was OK, and when I had turned fifteen, I went into hospital to have the baby. I had a little boy and called him Mick. They took him away from birth and put me into a children's home. They let me see Mick now and then. I had to get on with my life again. All the time I was fighting for the custody of Mick, but I was fighting a losing battle.

When I was seventeen I fell pregnant with my daughter, so I had to adopt-out Mick because I knew I was too young to look after two kids. By this time my brother and sisters were living in England and my stepdad was dead. I had no one to turn to so I had to go to the same mother-and-baby home with my daughter until the council got me a two bedroomed flat and I could move into it.

When I moved in I could not afford to live on what they gave me, so I went back onto the streets to work. It worked for a while then I had to go to prison. They took Charlotte into foster care. When I came out I got her back and I wrote to my brother in England and he came up to live with me and help me look after her. When he thought I could cope on my own he moved to England again. I was back to square one, on the streets, arrested, Charlotte in foster care again. This time it was longer and I lost my flat, so I took to the drink very heavy. But I still went to see her as much as possible.

Then one day when I was twenty years old and pregnant again, I looked at myself in the mirror and I didn't like what I saw. I decided to sort out my life before I lost another child. My next child was born, called Deidre. I got a house in Easterhouse with my brother, and I looked up an old friend who lived nearby and we became good friends and she helped me get some things for my house. Then she introduced me to her ex-bloke and we hit it off right away. Things were going great and I was on my way to getting Charlotte back. Ivor asked me to marry him and I said yes. My brother got a place of his own just around the corner.

Me and Ivor got married. I got Charlotte back and things were looking up for me for the first couple of years. Then Ivor started to drink very heavy. I wanted to pack mine and the girls' bags and leave, but I loved him so much and he needed us to help him through it so I stayed. I needed help too so I started to attend the Salvation Army. It was the best thing I had done in a long time. At first it was just me and the kids going then I talked Ivor into coming with me to see what it was like and he liked it. The Salvation Army meant the world to me. The holidays at Butlins − and we never went on holidays before. The kids going to the Sunday School. Christmas Day at the Sally was great. I was in the women's choir which Annette led. I never missed a Sunday service. Captain and Mrs Buchanan were a part of our life and they still are even though they have retired. I always remember the captain's bushy eyebrows. It helped me to believe in God. It took me a long time to accept. I do believe although sometimes I doubt. I think, if there is a God why have these things happened to me, why hasn't he prevented them? But it is not his fault that these things happen.

Ivor was still drinking. Then I fell pregnant with his son Gilbert. My brother moved back to England and we moved to a bigger flat. Things were tight moneywise, plus the girls were being picked on at school because they were of mixed race. Charlotte was getting the worst of it as she was the oldest. Then I fell pregnant again with another girl. A couple of months after her birth, my brother and my sister came from England for a holiday and they saw what was happening to the girls. They suggested that we all moved to England. They took the two girls with them back to England when they went back so that me and Ivor could settle things in Easterhouse.

We moved to a place called Wakefield, and it was hard because we had no money. We had to sleep here and there, then we went into a homeless people's hostel and we hated it. Then just after Christmas we got a letter from the council asking us to leave because we were not entitled to a house because we gave up one in Easterhouse. They just did not understand. So we were out on the streets yet again. We moved in with my brother in his one-bedroomed flat so that was three adults and four kids getting on top of each other. Then a letter came that we had been allocated a house of our own. Me and Ivor were dancing about, hugging each other we were just so happy.

We moved into the house with nothing. We had no money to buy things with. We put in to DHSS, but they could only give us so much and it was not enough to get half the things we needed, so my family chipped in to help us. It was still not enough, so we had to borrow money from all sorts of places. The girls were getting picked on at school again, plus Charlotte was attacked by a man. It was all getting on top of me and I just don't know how I coped.

My friend Bet came to England to live with us in

Wakefield. Then she got a bedsit in Bradford and I would go and visit her. When I saw that it was full of different coloured people I thought of moving there so that the girls could be in amongst their own type. By this time, Charlotte was thirteen and Deidre was ten. We were told by Bet's landlord that if we moved into one of his rooms for a couple of days then he would give me the keys to a four-bedroom house. He took us to look at the house and we loved it at first sight. So we moved to Bradford into one room. Then he was called to Pakistan so we were stuck in this one room, six of us in one double bed. Ivor was helping out at the chip shop at the back of our building. But he was getting pennies for it. He would drink a lot because he could not cope with it all. Neither could I so I ended up taking an overdose which almost killed me.

When I got out of the hospital, I got in touch with social services. They sent this woman to our room and she was hopeless and offered no help at all. So when she went away I got in touch with them again and asked for someone else to help me. They sent a lady called Lorraine, and she was a great help to us all. She asked me what I wanted her to do, so we sat and talked for a bit. I explained how I came to be in Bradford, and she asked if I wanted her to take the kids into care till she helped me get a house. I told her it would break my heart but it was for the best. So I let her take the three big ones and I kept the youngest one with me. It was so hard, but I knew the kids were well cared for and I saw them a lot. But Ivor was still drinking. Then my brother moved to Bradford beside me which was a bit of a help. I got an offer of a lovely four-bedroomed house. When we went to see it I was head over heels with it. I would have been daft to turn it down so I accepted it and Lorraine helped me get the grant for it.

I moved in on the Wednesday and got the kids home on the Monday which was a bit quick because I was not quite right in the head. I did not know what was happening to me because not long before we moved into the house my thirteen-year-old daughter Charlotte was raped by some Asian boy and it broke my heart. So when we moved in and the kids came home I could not cope, and me and Ivor were not getting on at all. I asked him to leave, then I started to drink very heavy and I was smoking drugs. It all started getting on top of me, so I asked Lorraine to take the kids back into care till I sorted my head out, and she did. Again I saw them all the time. So did Ivor. I was still drinking a lot, then Ivor came to have a talk with me and asked if we could go back to normal. But I was not ready as my head was still in a mess. I let him move back into the house, but he had to sleep in one of the kids' beds. I could see for myself that I was hurting him in a bad way. But I could not help myself. Then one night I realized how much we were missing the kids. So we talked about getting our lives sorted out and getting the kids back for good. So we did and it was fine for a bit. Then Ivor started to drink again because the job he was doing was not getting paid right. It went on for a couple of years. The worst was when he would come in drunk and speak to me the way he did. I know he didn't mean it but it still hurt me to hear him. I wanted to leave and be on my own, but he needed me bad. So did the kids as they had been through enough, so I had to put up with it the best I could. People would say they don't know how I coped. Neither did I. Then one day he was caught drinking and driving. He lost his licence and he was fined. With all that was happening, he had a nervous breakdown and he was taken into a mental hospital for a bit. Now things are a lot better between us. He doesn't drink now although he does get depressed a lot. But we have learnt to cope with it the best we can. The only problem we have now is the same as always and that is MONEY. I show this by keeping a diary.

**Monday**
I got up and got the kids dressed for school and gave them some tea and toast. Charlotte went to the post office to collect the child benefit. I gave Deidre £2.80 for two days' bus fares to school and back. Went to shop and spent money like this.

    0.69   5lb potatoes
    0.69   loaf
    5.00   gas token
    5.03   cigs, tobacco, cig papers
    0.60   2 tins beans
    0.22   soap
    0.49   washing-up liquid

Had a quick nap before I started on the kids' tea. When they came home from school, Gilbert and Mary needed money for school Christmas trips but I don't have it to give to them. I can't even start thinking about Christmas presents for the kids. I can't go to the DHSS because I already owe them so much. We watched some TV then we all went to bed.

**Tuesday**
Got the kids up and to school. Spend money on

|       |                                |
|-------|--------------------------------|
| 0.69  | potatoes                       |
| 0.60  | 2 tins beans                   |
| 0.69  | bread                          |
| 5.03  | cigs, tobacco, cig papers      |
| 0.73  | 2lb sugar                      |
| 1.98  | soap powder                    |
| 1.77  | 2 packets of toilet towels     |
| 0.67  | packet of toilet rolls         |
| 1.40  | ticket for Deidre for tomorrow |

I am left with £1.00. I get a letter from the Water Board, they say that they are going to cut me off. I keep the £1 for the kids so they can get some sweets from the shops. It is not much but it will keep them happy for a little while. Made the tea, watched TV, then we all went to bed early.

**Wednesday**
Got up with the kids. Made them tea and toast and got them off to school. Peace at last. Charlotte went to the post office to get our social money. £74.49. Spend money on

|       |            |
|-------|------------|
| 10.00 | gas token  |
| 10.00 | electric   |

5.00   water token
4.87   cigs and tobacco
5.18   milk
0.69   bread
0.69   potatoes
0.49   marg
1.96   2 packets of Scotch pies
0.60   2 tins beans
1.40   Deidre's bus ticket

I have spent £40.96 and have £33.53 left. Gilbert is off school at the moment because he needs new shoes and that is £10. I can't afford them just now so I will have to wait and see what I can do for him. The kids come home from school. Thank God they get a meal at school.

Ivor is making the tea while I get the kids ready for bed. Deidre and Charlotte are going out with some friends. So me and Ivor are on our own at last for the first time in ages. The kids come back and we all went to bed.

## Thursday

Up with kids again. No rest for the wicked. It is Halloween tonight. I can't afford to get things in so I will keep the door locked when other kids knock. I hate to do it but I have no option. The kids want to go out for the night, but I don't like the idea that they are taking from people and I can't give in return. But they keep going on and on so I told them to do what they want. So they are off to school now. Me and Charlotte are doing the housework, it is all I seem to do. Ivor got up for about ten minutes and went back to bed. Charlotte went to the shops for tea and bought

| | |
|---|---|
| 0.69 | loaf |
| 0.69 | potatoes |
| 2.97 | cigarettes |
| 1.28 | 1 doz eggs |
| 0.60 | 2 tins beans |
| 1.98 | packet of sausages |
| 1.40 | bus ticket |

I have £23.92 left.

The kids are home from school so I am making the tea and Charlotte is getting them ready to go out. Mary is a witch and Gilbert is a woman and they look good dressed up. So me and Ivor have the whole house to ourselves for a couple of hours. We listened to some music and played draughts. Then the kids came home, got washed and into bed. They said they had fun so they went right to sleep. Ivor and me watched some TV then went to bed.

**Friday**
Up with the kids, made them tea and toast, off to school. Got on with the cleaning and housework. Ivor is depressed today, a bit more than usual, so he is staying in bed all day. Charlotte went to the shops and got

| | |
|---|---|
| 0.69 | bread |
| 0.69 | potatoes |
| 0.49 | marg |

1.09    10 frozen hamburgers
0.60    2 tins beans
0.23    soap
1.40    ticket for Deidre

I have £18.73 left. Kids came home from school. I'll
make a tea of hamburgers, chips and beans. Kids and me
play cards and draughts and then we watch TV for a while
then off to bed with them. That leaves me on my own so
I am off for a bath and then bed.

## Saturday
We all had a bit of a sleep in this morning then I made
them some toast. The kids went out to play. I have a bit
of a headache and feel sick but I can't go back to bed
because someone has to look after the kids so I just have
to soldier on. I sent Charlotte for the tea things:

0.69    bread
0.69    potatoes
5.00    electric token
2.93    cigs
0.60    2 tins beans
1.77    3 tins meat balls
1.98    box soap powder

I've got £5.07 left. I need another gas token because it is
so cold in this house, but I can't afford it this week. I lay
on the couch for a bit but it did not last long because
there is some cleaning to do. Tea time again. We are
having mashed potatoes and meat balls in gravy. Then we

did the washing up and we all sat and watched a film on TV. We all went to bed early.

## Sunday

I didn't want to get up today because I felt so fed up with my life. It's the same thing day-in, day-out. I don't get to go out with Ivor or on my own because we can't afford it. I don't know the last time we went out together. We don't get to go on holiday. The last time we went away was when we lived in Easterhouse with the Salvation Army to Butlin's holiday camp. That was seven years ago. Enough of my moaning. The kids are running about mad wanting their tea and toast. Charlotte goes to the shops.

| | |
|---|---|
| 0.69 | bread |
| 0.69 | potatoes |
| 1.38 | 2 tins corned beef |
| 0.60 | 2 tins beans |
| 1.50 | 10 cigarettes |

I have 21p left. The kids have been out playing while I got their school clothes washed and make tea. Then it is into the bath for them for school tomorrow and off to bed.

I am sitting on my own again and I said a little prayer asking for a little guidance. Then I went to bed.

## Monday

Up with kids for school. Made tea and toast for them. Gilbert is still off school because he has no shoes. I can't help it but on Wednesday I'll go round the secondhand shops to see what I can do because I must get him back to school quick. Mary and Deidre are off to school and Mary needed 80p for school. Charlotte is off to the post office to get the child benefit which is £28.61. She then went to the shop for me.

| | |
|------|---------------------------------|
| 0.69 | bread |
| 0.89 | tea bags |
| 0.73 | sugar |
| 0.49 | marg |
| 0.69 | potatoes |
| 0.60 | 2 tins beans |
| 1.38 | dozen eggs |
| 5.03 | cigarettes, tobacco and cig paper |
| 5.00 | gas token, at last |
| 1.40 | bus ticket for Deidre |

I have £10.21 left. The kids came home from school. They went to play in the back yard while I make the tea, chips and eggs and beans. They ate their tea and then got ready for bed and they watched TV with me and we went to bed.

## Tuesday

Up for school again. Made the kids tea and toast and sent them to school. Charlotte and me cleaned out the house. Then we had a rest before she went to the shop for some things.

| | |
|------|--------------|
| 0.69 | bread |
| 0.60 | 2 tins beans |

0.69   potatoes
2.93   cigs
1.40   2 tins hot dogs
1.40   Deidre's bus fares

I now have £2.90 left. Sitting on my own for a bit watching the afternoon TV. Dozed off, woke up with a very sore head, but the kids are due in from school any minute. Mary is watching cartoons. Deidre is listening to music. Gilbert is cleaning his room. Charlotte is helping me do the tea. Ivor is in his bed. Tea is over, the kids are getting ready for bed. I am washing-up. We are going to watch TV then it's off to bed for the kids. Now I am on my own. It's a bit boring because all you can hear is lots of fireworks and bangers. It is November 5th. I am off to bed.

**Wednesday**
Got up. I get the kids dressed. I feed the kids breakfast and I send Ivor's up to him in bed because he spends most of his time in bed with his sore back plus he suffers from very bad depression. He ended up in hospital once with it. So most of the time I am on my own with the kids. Charlotte went to the post office for me. The hill to the post office is too much for me. I have two books. One is reserved for the money-lenders because I owe a lot and so I don't see any of that. Charlotte comes back with my money from the other book. It is £74.49. I spend

10.00   gas token
10.00   electric

5.00    water
4.40    cigarettes and tobacco
0.69    loaf
0.49    marg
0.69    half a dozen eggs

I am left with £43.22. The kids are out playing with friends because they are off school for ten days. I am doing a bit of housework. Now I am reading some magazines I got from the day centre.

Charlotte has to go to town, 1.60 bus fare. She is back and she is going to the shop to get some dinner. I need quite a lot.

0.69    5lb potatoes
0.69    loaf
0.73    2lb sugar
1.92    soap powder
0.60    2 tins beans
0.86    tea bags

I have £36.13 left. Now I'll make the kids some dinner, which is beans on toast. Nothing to do but sit and watch TV. Tea time. Send for some fish fingers and beans which cost £2.56 so I've got £33.57. I make the kids their tea and get them ready for bed and watch some more TV. Ivor comes down for about an hour with us then back to bed for him. Then it's time for the kids' bed. Now I am on my own again so I go out to the path and stand for about five or ten minutes, come in and watch more TV. Now it's time for my bed.

## Thursday
Up with the kids again. Send to the shops for bread to make the kids some tea and toast for breakfast. Sent some up to Ivor. Get the kids ready.

    0.69   bread

Now left with £32.88. The kids are out to play, then they sit and watch TV with me. Dozed off for about half an hour then woke up with the kids fighting amongst themselves. I feel ill, I go to see the doctor at the day centre. I have to get the bus, which costs £1.60.

    0.69   loaf
    1.80   tobacco for Ivor
    0.89   box of 12 frozen hamburgers

I have £27.90 left.

I came home and had to clean up after the kids because the place was in a hell of a mess. A woman's work is never done. So to tea, chips and burgers, then washing-up. I get the kids ready for bed. Not seen Ivor today, he's been in bed all this time. I'll have a bath then off to bed. I have to go and see a social worker tomorrow because I want to start looking for my son who was adopted out when he was two years old and I was just seventeen.

## Friday
Got up and sent for some bread and marge. Made the kids some toast. Got ready to go to the social workers. Spent

0.69   bread
0.49   marge
1.90   tobacco
0.20   cig papers
0.69   5lb potatoes
5.18   milkman
1.80   bus fare to social work

I have £16.95 left. After I came home I cleaned up and Ivor got up for a little while and we talked about how I got on at the social services. I told him that if I want to register with the adoption agency I have to find £27 to register. But I don't have that kind of money and there is no one left to help me because I owe them a lot as it is. So I will just have to wait and see what happens with my adopted son.

I made some tea for the kids, sent for a dozen eggs and some beans, which came to £2.58 so leaving £14.37. Deidre came in with her friend and asked if she could go to the disco, but I had to tell her no because the money is tight. She was not pleased but she had to go along with it. Then we all sat and watched a film on TV before we went to bed.

## Saturday

Got up as usual but my head hurts so bad. The kids are running about mad so I had to shout at them, so they were not pleased with me at all. Made them some toast. I had to send for bread plus some cigs. Must have my cigs or I can't get through the day. I hate it that people say that because you are on social security you shouldn't smoke.

But it's like Valium, it calms me. I wish I could give it up. I have tried and failed.

    0.69   bread
    2.93   cigs
    5.00   electric token

I have £5.75 left. I have asked the kids to help clean up for me. They moaned but they did it. We all sat and watched TV. The TV set is on its last legs and I don't know what I'd do without it.

The kids asked for some bread. I could only give them one slice each because it is all that was left. Ivor has not got up today.

Me, Deidre and Charlotte had a game of cards and I won. The kids went to bed. I wanted to go for a bath but I have to keep the hot water for Sunday for the kids.

We had mashed potatoes and meat balls for tea.

    0.69   potatoes
    0.98   two tins meat balls

I have £4.08 left. I am off to bed now.

## Sunday
Got up with the kids as usual. From the shop got

    0.69   bread
    0.35   salt
    0.69   5lb potatoes

0.60    2 tins beans
1.58    2 tins chopped ham

Just a few pence left. I need some gas but I don't have enough so we will just have to put up with the cold till morning. It is quite cold in the house.

The kids look for their school clothes so that I can wash them. We just sit and watch TV till it's time for tea. Charlotte helps to make the tea which is a big help, and then we wash up together and she puts things away while I run the bath. In goes Mary then Gilbert and off to bed for them.

Ivor got up for a couple of hours, so we watched TV and played cards then we went to bed.

I am not rich and I am not angry about it. I am the worst off in this street. Next door has some beautiful things. I don't hold a grudge against them, I'm glad they have got it. But I don't like it to be rubbed in like when other people's kids boast to my kids, 'We've got this, you haven't.' It does make me jealous at times. I don't want to be stinking rich. I just want to be comfortable so that when my kids want a new pair of shoes, I can buy a pair. I had to go to a secondhand shop to get Gilbert a pair so he could get back to school. I've got central heating but I can't afford to turn it on. I am still in debt paying for last Christmas. I am still paying for the kids' clothes. Sometimes you have to borrow to eat. Once I lent from a man and put down my child benefit book. I worked out that he took £450 to lend me £220 for Christmas. It was robbery but I had no other option. I don't have much time for politics, I've got my kids to look after. But I do think everyone should be equal. I hope my children have a better future. I would not part with my kids or with my husband. But if I had my time again I would not have so many kids. I don't like the poverty, I don't like the kids coming home and asking for something and I can't give it to them.

# Anita

**29 May 1993**

Six years ago, I had six children and was eight and a half months pregnant. We had been living in Castlemilk, a big scheme in Glasgow. We were a happy family. My husband Arnold was on sickness benefit and I was on income support. We managed and even had a few luxuries. Arnold would take the children to the park and for walks. I would buy the food out of my money, and if the children needed anything like clothes or shoes he would keep his income for them. Then we moved to Easterhouse.

One Tuesday he was out for several hours. I asked him why he had been so long and accused him of drinking. One thing led to another and I told him to get out and not come back. He asked me if I really meant it and I said yes. Arnold went and got dressed and all the time I was saying to myself, 'Don't go, Arnold, please stay.' But I had too much pride to tell him. He stood at the door and asked, 'You don't want me any more?' I never answered but inside I was saying. 'I do, I love you.' He said, 'If you don't want me, I'm going to do myself in.' I replied, 'You do that,' not thinking he would.

I never saw him again. I did not report him missing until Friday. I thought he had gone to his sister and was staying away to give me a fright. The police came and asked if he had any marks or tattoos. I told them he had my name on his arm.

The next day I went to the hospital to be induced. I was in the ward for just one hour when a nurse took me into a room where my brother was with a doctor and policeman. The doctor said, 'Anita, your husband is not alive.' Arnold had thrown himself into the River Clyde. I just screamed. Then I was in labour. It was the only birth that Arnold did not see.

Since Arnold died I have just been existing and taking one day at a time. I was left with seven children. Peter was fifteen, Cheryl fourteen, Susan thirteen, Bill eight, Angie six, Morris four and Maureen just a few days old.

I could not tell the children about their dad. The three eldest knew but just could not accept it. Peter turned to drugs. Someone told him it would help him to forget. I suppose it did for a while. I did not know what to do after losing my husband and just having a baby, I felt I was losing my son as well. Arnold would have done anything for his children, he would play with them and take them out, all the things that I don't do. My children must have been going through hell, I just could not cope without him. I kept thinking, what am I going to do, how am I going to live without him. I just could not cope. I should have been giving my kids love and lots of cuddles because I knew they must be hurting very bad inside wondering what had happened to their dad. One of my sisters told the three small ones that their daddy had had an accident and was in heaven. All I heard was them crying and asking lots of questions. All I could tell them was that they would see their dad again when they went to sleep and they would dream about him but they did not understand. Bill was very withdrawn because his dad always played football with him and took him to see Celtic. Bill knows that his dad brought him his first ball as soon as he could walk. My daughter Susan was very close to her dad, all the children were, they were closer to Arnold than with me. He had more patience with them and if they had anything they wanted to know about or talk about they went to him. Arnold was the one who had to tell my two daughters about the facts of life when they menstruated. I couldn't talk about things like that as I was brought up in a very strict family and thought it was dirty.

My daughter, Susan, just could not cope with her dad not being here. Arnold had delivered her in the house and there was a bond between them. She ran away two months after he died and was away for a full week before the police found her in Nottingham looking for her Uncle Joe (my brother). The week she was away, I just wanted to die. I kept thinking that it was me being punished for what I did. I felt Arnold was going to take the kids one by one away from me. Susan was out of my control and had to be put into care as did Cheryl. It broke my heart to do that. I did not want my girls turning to drugs to forget, which I knew might have happened if I kept them in Easterhouse. But everything has worked out great for my two girls, Susan and Cheryl. Susan is working with the elderly and Cheryl models in her spare time when she is not working.

My heart aches for my son Peter who, I suspect, is still

taking drugs. But he is a tower of strength to me. My four schoolchildren still talk about Arnold, except little Maureen. I know that their dad's death has affected them badly. Bill became withdrawn, Morris turned from a lovely, well-behaved boy and ended up having problems at school. He was only three and a half when Arnold died, but he still remembers the last day he had out with his dad. Their school work has suffered and their behaviour in school. I have been to children's panels because of my depressions and not wanting to go on any more. I would not let anyone in the house, and I would not go out. I have no social life. My children hardly go out of Easterhouse. I cannot afford to give them the things they need like nice clothes and nice bedrooms. I would love them to have all these things and to take them on holidays, but it is impossible on social security. It is very hard to make ends meet. I get paid on a Monday, and by the end of the week I have got to ask Bob if he can lend me anything, which he does. Bob lives nearby and runs a boys' club called Covenanters. He has become a good friend and takes Bill to camp every year.

When Arnold died, he took half of me with him. I thought the pain would ease, but I will never get over it. I keep asking myself why did I argue with him over some trivial thing?

All my family have been left terribly scarred by their dad's death. I don't bother about myself, it is my kids that I would like to give the things that other children have. I wish I could win the pools, but I know it will never happen. I just keep wishing and dreaming it would. I have not had much of a life myself, but my children have been through much worse. They deserve a better life than they have had. I manage to get by and to feed the kids but that is all. I think about just giving up, but if I did anything to myself, what would happen to my kids? They are all I have and I love them with all my heart. I know I would be with Arnold. Sometimes I say to myself, why not just do it and take the children with me, at least we would all be out of this misery and poverty because I know things will remain the way they are and nobody is going to change it. I sit and think all the time what I can do for the best.

## 17 February 1994

My morning starts by getting the children up for school. They don't eat in the morning before they go, but I make sure they have a packet of crisps and a quenchie for their tuck, although I have got to either ask the van or borrow for it.

I like telling the truth. Sometimes I am too depressed to get up in the morning and I rely on my teenage son, Bill, to get Morris and Maureen dressed for school, and he takes them there and goes and collects them. I don't wake up in the best of moods and I take it out on the children. It is not their fault, the problem is me. My feelings are all mixed up. I am full of anger and guilt. Angry at Arnold leaving me to cope on my own and for what he did. Guilt because I blame myself for what happened to Arnold but most of all guilt for taking it out on my kids.

It is now 9.30 and the house is very quiet. When the

house is quiet like this I say to myself I am going to hug my kids and tell them how much I love them. But when the time comes, I can't, but I think they know I love them. My heart goes out to them because they have suffered a lot with losing their dad. I am going to get dressed and wait for Bob as I promised him and I can't let him down.

My friend Bob Holman called round and is trying to help my daughter, Susan, get a pram. She is due to have her first baby next week. I promised to go with him to look for a secondhand pram in Motherwell.

In the afternoon, I went with Bob to Motherwell and I enjoyed myself very much. Susan liked the pram that Bob got for her. I don't feel so good just now because I had a silly argument with Susan over something trivial.

I have nothing in for the kids' supper after helping Susan. It is at times like this when I have no food that I am at my lowest. I am going to send Bill along to Bob's to see if he can give me enough for supper, I feel terrible asking but he is the only one I can turn to. Morris and Maureen are out playing and Angie is at her dancing club. Peter was going to go out for a little while, but I asked him to sit in with me. To me he is the best son a mother could have. When Bill gets back, I will give the kids something to eat, get them washed and watch TV for a little while. I do not have a video or I would let them watch a film. It is hard telling them I can't afford one, but maybe one day.

I say my prayers tonight as I do every night. I will be asking God to try and make our lives a little better. Although I don't go to chapel very often, I have never missed saying my prayers at night. I have doubted God in the past when I have went through some very bad times. But when I feel like that I write and tell Mother Rosary how I feel, and what she tells me is always right. I think everybody doubts God when something bad happens to them, it is because they feel angry at a loved one being taken from them, and they wonder if there really is a God and he lets this happen to them. Only God knows, and I know that everybody who has suffered in this life will have a better life when it is our time to go. I am looking forward to going because I know I will see Arnold again, and my mother. It is all I have to look forward to, but I hope all my kids are grown up when God wants me.

I am a Roman Catholic. I was in a convent children's home for three years when I was young. I wanted to be a nun, and if all my children were grown up I would go into a convent. I believe I was meant to be a nun, and it was my ambition since I was a little girl.

## 19 February 1994

Yesterday I was feeling down and stayed in my bed all day just thinking about what lies ahead for my kids. Morris has been missing some school but went back yesterday and that made me feel better.

Today has been fine, but just like any other day, it is the same old routine. Angie passed her dancing exams and I am very happy for her and hope she keeps it up and does not lose interest as it is the only thing going for her. Bill is staying with his aunt tonight, and it seems funny in the house without him. Bill is fifteen next month. He has got a lot of talent at sport, especially football and table tennis, and I would not like it to go to waste. But living in Easterhouse with money problems all the time, there is not much hope for him.

Some people say that money is the root of all evil. But if I had just enough to help my kids, it would be like a gift from heaven. It can't be evil if you put it to good use and see the happiness in the kids' faces, even if it is just a little thing they have always wanted. Well, tomorrow is another day.

## 22 February 1994

I have not been feeling too well due to women's troubles. Today has been fine but I am really getting worried about Morris at school. There seems to be something worrying him. He is all right at home, it is just when he is at school. I had to go to an attendance meeting tonight because of his attendance. It is quite bad and I was unaware that he has been off so many times. To tell the truth, I would not have attended if Bob did not come for me. Morris told me that I had missed it and that it was held last night so Bob saved the day. When I came back from the meeting I asked Morris about the times he had stayed away from school, he admitted staying off and his reason was that the headteacher kept getting him into trouble. I know Morris can be a stubborn wee boy at times, but when he is spoken nicely to or shown an extra bit of attention he is totally different. I promised him an extra 50p onto his pocket money if he behaves at school and I was paying him more attention than I usually do, and I could see that maybe that is where the problem lies because his wee face lit up when I was talking to him about everyday things and telling him how important it is to me that he is good in and out of school, and he promises me that this time he is going to be good.

It is amazing that by just giving Morris that little extra special attention how different he is because he is just used to hearing me shouting or just sitting not talking to him or any of my children. It is so very hard bringing children up on your own. I can't give them a father's love and I know that they miss that. I promise to myself that from tonight I will have to take more interest in my kids and talk kindly to them more often because I saw what a difference it made to Morris tonight when I was taking an interest in his writing and talking to him about school. I don't usually do that, he is so used to me raising my voice to him when he gets into trouble at school, but I am going to do my best and change things.

It is because I am so full of anger that I tend to take it out on my children but never physically. Nobody knows how I feel except myself because I can't talk to anybody about it. It is getting late so I will carry on writing tomorrow. I have another meeting tomorrow at school concerning Morris's behaviour so I will see what tomorrow brings. I know if I keep my promise to my children and pay them more attention it will show in their behaviour. I am sure the teachers will see a difference in Morris if they could only see the other side to him and not the bad boy that misbehaves at school. I am sure that through time they will see the good boy in him and I hope it is in the near future.

Angie is fourteen now. I worry about her. She was only six when Arnold went away but she can still remember him. I feel so angry at myself for getting on at her as I do. Sometimes I shout at her for nothing. I know she needs a lot of love and attention from me, and I would do anything to give her it. I would like nothing more than to sit Angie beside me and cuddle her and tell how much I love her, but I can't show my feelings that way. I can write them down and say them to myself but what use is that when my children just want me to tell them how much they mean to me? I blame the way I was brought up for being like this. I can't remember getting a cuddle when I was young although I knew my mam and dad loved me. But they never told me and maybe that is just what I needed. If I had been given this in my childhood maybe I would be able to give my children the love and attention they so desperately need. I have tried telling the kids my feelings and they say it is all right, but I know it is not, everybody needs to know they are loved. I don't want my children to be the same as me and not be able to show their feelings to their children.

I am going to write to Mother Rosary and ask her what kind of girl I was at the ages thirteen to fifteen when I was in the convent. I want to know if I was able to tell her my feelings and things that were bothering me. I want to know if I had confidence in myself and if I got on all right with other children in the convent. I can remember things like missing my mam and dad and brothers and sisters. I remember crying myself to sleep at night wanting my mam and dad. As the months passed, I got used to it and I came to love Mother Rosary as I loved my own mam. She was my mother for three years and that is why I love her very much.

## 23 February 1994

It is teatime, 5.30. I went up to the school today for the meeting concerning Morris's behaviour. I did not think it would be so hurtful listening to four strangers talking about my son. I was really angry, you would think that Morris was a real terror. It is times like this when I really need Arnold and I get so angry at him for not being here to support me and his children. Then again, if he was here Morris's behaviour would not be as it is just now. Morris behaves just like any other boy. If he was quiet and withdrawn then I would start to worry. I know myself deep down that within the month we will see a different boy. I have been talking to him quite a lot and it seems to be doing the trick.

I love my children very much more than anything in this world, and I would do anything to protect them. Tomorrow is a special day for my little girl Maureen, she invited her grandpa (my father) up to school for a cup of tea and she is very excited because she has not seen him for some time. I only hope my dad is well enough to come as he is nearly seventy. I don't think he will let her down as he is very close to all his family and grandchildren, but I think Maureen is his favourite and she loves him. He is the only man Maureen is very close to, she did not know her own dad as she was just born when Arnold died and looks upon my dad as a father figure. So tomorrow is a big day for her, her wee face lights up when I talk to her about him and she wonders why I don't take her down to stay with him. When she gets older I will explain to her that grandad is getting old and has had his turn at bringing up seventeen children of his own. I know my dad would welcome us with open arms, but he is used to being in the house with my young brother Albert all the time and it would take some getting used to children running about again.

I don't know how my mother coped with fifteen kids (two died) as my dad was a seaman and was often away for several months at a time. She must have had the patience of a saint, and I can say this, none of us were angels. I have seven brothers and seven sisters and we are a close-knit family. My father was very strict when we were young, but when he went back to sea I will always remember crying in my bed at night hoping he would come home soon. My mam used to say to me when you see a big white eagle then you will know your dad's ship is in. Sometimes she was right. He used to call me his duchess and he still does to this day. Thinking back, my mam had her worries, especially with the boys, they were lovable rogues. I will always remember the things they got up to. My mam must have went through something similar to what I am going through just now. How she got by without my dad I don't know. God must have been guiding her. It wasn't just the boys that got into trouble, we girls were just as bad. But I remember we were a happy family. I loved bedtime, there was about five in one bed and what a laugh we used to get, all of us in one big room telling stories and carrying on, it was great. I remember when my mam used to get her pay. My dad would send her an allotment note £14 every fortnight. I don't know why they called it that but how she managed to feed and clothe all of us on £14 God only knows. She is an inspiration to me. All I can say is, when she died God must have wanted a new big flower for his garden. She is resting now which is something I never saw her do, she was always washing over the sink or cleaning up. She hardly ever sat down, and us kids were always up to something. She must have missed my dad very much but never showed it. She just kept herself busy. We were a right handful but I had a happy childhood and a wonderful mother and father. I used to pine a lot for my dad. I never saw any of my brothers or sisters crying for him. Maybe they did and I never saw it, but I think I was the worst. Every mum and dad have their favourite and I was my dad's. My brother Joe was my mum's, I think it was because he was her first boy. She loved us all equally, but Joe was that little bit special. I will carry on tomorrow as I feel sad just now thinking back and how hard it must have been for my mam. I hope she is watching over me just now.

**24 February 1994**

Another day, the kids are off to school. Peter is still sleeping and Bill is making himself a bit of toast. I am feeling fine this morning. It was good to think back about my childhood and all the good memories. I have some bad ones and sad ones, but the good ones overpower the bad.

Before my mother and father moved to Royston, we stayed at 14, Gray Street, Anderston. I must have only been about six or seven but I can remember vividly the wee 'single end'[2] we stayed in. There was only two beds in it, one was for us kids and the other for my mam and dad. But when dad went to sea, my mam would take some of us beside her. We all had different turns at sleeping with her. There was six of us living in that wee single end. I did not have good memories about Gray Street. I always felt very lonely and missed my dad very much. He must have been at sea all the time and I can only remember seeing him occasionally. Then we moved to Royston, a four-apartment. My dad still lives there now.

**25 February 1994**

I was about six years old when my family moved house, and the house we moved to was like a big mansion compared to our wee single end. It had three bedrooms and a kitchen, which we called the scullery, and an inside toilet with a bath. We all loved it.

My dad still went to sea and these were the worst times. This was in the 1950s and we were poor. My mam never took any drink until she was thirty and, when my dad was away, my uncles would come up and urge her to take a drink. When my dad came home on leave, it was great. My mam was happy, you could see it in her face. Dad was always loaded with presents for us – big dolls, watches, clothes. None of my mam's brothers and sisters then came up so often as my dad did not get on very well with them because he knew they would give my mam a drink and my Uncle Philip and Uncle Dave would talk my mam into selling our clothes and toys. They stayed with us at times when dad was away. I loved the uncles. Uncle Philip used to sit me on his knee and sing songs that he had written. He used to learn me them, and to this day I still remember parts of one of them,

You are my darling,
the essence of shining,
You are my sweetheart,
you're my everything.
But now that I know
what I never knew,
I'm in heaven,
when I am with you.

*Chorus*
You hoo, I love you,
My darling I do.

I will never forget these words and the tune of the song as I used to sing along with him.

My dad did not like my mum's brothers, except one or two. They fought with my dad a lot. Mam and dad, like any married couple, had their arguments, and sometimes my mam would end up with a mark on her which her brothers did not like and they would start on my dad. I detested hearing mam and dad fighting and was scared. I was glad when dad stopped going to sea and stayed at home with all of us. He would have his pint on Friday. My mam just went out on odd times with my dad but mostly she never left the house. When dad was out at the weekend, she would sit at the window with her bottle of Guinness waiting on my dad coming, not knowing whether he would be in a good mood or a bad one. I can remember when our electricity was cut off and my mum always had to buy candles. She used to cook our meals on the fire. I was about eight and it would be 1958 or 1959. There were hundreds of other families like us. Today is no different. I think it is worse. At least I had my mam and dad and brothers and sisters. We were hungry at times but my mam always made sure we never went without. She always managed to get something.

**26 February 1994**

I think today is worse than the 1950s. I can't get by from week to week without borrowing. I don't like asking people. I always get one of the kids to ask for me. The Social Work Department is there for deprived families and there are hundreds in Easterhouse. I know that some families do get holidays and clothes from them, but myself and the children have never been offered things. I did once ask the department for help. It was very hard, I had to swallow my pride, I felt as though I was begging. I felt very degraded and low when they refused me. Nobody knows how bad I was feeling after being turned down. I have no liking for social workers as they have done nothing for my kids. Bob is the only one who has taken my kids on holiday.

## 17 June 1995

I have not been writing for over a year, but I just have to get my feelings and anger out and the only way I can do that is to write it down. It has not been a good year for myself and my children. I feel like giving up. I don't think I can cope much longer. Everyday things are harder for me. I have been at a children's panel and I was told if I needed any help just to let my social worker know. Just yesterday I had nothing at all for my kids to eat and I called the social worker but it was just a blunt 'no'.

On Monday morning, 12 June, I was taken out of my house by the police for an educational warrant, because my son, Bill, was not attending school. But Bill had been told by the social worker that he did not have to go back to school. I was fined £75 and my son, Peter, had to come down and take £75 out of my income support to get me home. I had no money left and I was so angry at the social worker for not trying to get me some food for the kids that I told him to come and take them away. He refused to do that as well. I did not want my children taken away from me but I was just so mad at being refused help. I told him I would end up doing something to myself if I could not get any food. Some people don't realize what it is like to see their children hungry. It is heartbreaking. My kids are now under social work supervision but I can't get no help or sympathy from them.

Bill has left home to stay with my daughter, Susan, because he doesn't want to stay in Easterhouse any more because of all the drugs. He wants to work. I desperately want away from this place for my kids' sake and to try to give them a better life.

Poverty is a terrible thing. I just cannot cope with what I am getting on income support. I just wish I could feed and clothe my children but it is impossible with what I receive.

## 10 September 1995

It is Sunday. The past few months have not been very good ones although there have been happy times. My wee Maureen made her first Holy Communion and she was beautiful. It was a very big day for her and she was all excited. She could not wait to get her lovely white dress on. I was very proud walking up to chapel with her. During Mass, I remember saying to myself, 'Arnold, if only you could see your little girl now. The baby you were so looking forward to being born but you were not here when she was born. You went away on 16 September and your little one was born four days later. She was very like you.' Maureen is no trouble at all, but she can be a little rascal at times. She loves school and does her homework.

## 27 January 1996

It's Saturday night, ten o'clock and I am at my dad's. I stayed overnight and will stay tonight as he has been ill. He is seventy-one years old. He is better now but still weak. I know he will be back to his old self soon. Angie and Maureen are here and Maureen is over the moon as she has been on at me all week to see her grandpa.

My brother, Albert, was out and my dad went to his bed. Albert came in quite late and had been drinking. I told him to keep his voice down as dad was sleeping but he did not listen to me. I don't talk much to Albert now, yet at one time we were quite close. I thought I could tell him things in confidence until just recently I found out different. There are two sides to Albert. When he is good, he is like a tonic and always makes me laugh. The other side I can't understand, like saying things behind my back.

**10 March 1996**

I am really worried about the kids growing up in Easterhouse. I want them away from here as things are getting worse. Bill is not working just now and I am terrified for him in case he gets in with the wrong crowd. My money problems are not getting better. I am only getting £52.30 weekly and £27.60 child benefit. My income support is low because money is deducted to pay back loans to the social security for things like beds and bedding, cooker and washing machine. I had to have them. I don't think they should be loans. In my opinion a grant should be given for important things. I can hardly feed my kids let alone clothe them, yet I know there is no point in applying for another loan for clothes. I just wish that somebody with enough influence could do something about it. I don't think the Social Work Department are any better, I have never had any help from them. It worries me sick wondering where the next meal is coming from. I get paid on a Monday, and by the time Thursday comes I sometimes have nothing.

I dread to think what the future holds for my kids if I don't get away from Easterhouse soon while they are still young, I know in my heart that they will either turn to drugs or end up in prison. My kids keep asking to move. They are lovely kids and intelligent and I would dearly love to see them making something of themselves. Maureen is very clever for her age, eight, and I don't want her growing up in this environment. But what can I do with no money? My children don't stand a chance. I don't think it is fair. There are hundreds of millionaires in this world but thousands living in poverty. When I pray at night, I ask why one person is better off than others and why God put us on this earth. Certainly it cannot be to make one person better than another but that is the way that it is just now – the rich and the poor. Why, as we are all equal?

**11 March 1996**

It is Monday morning and the kids are off to school. I am sitting in my bedroom as my two brothers and Peter's friends are in the living room. I just can't get used to anybody else staying in the house, even if it is my own brothers, let alone Peter's friends.

Morris and Maureen like Mondays because I give them £1 pocket money. It is all I can give them and they are happy with it.

I have been very excited since Sunday. Claire who works for FARE came to see me and gave me some phone numbers for a house away from here and near my daughters. There are private landlords with furnished rooms in safe places and you have to put down a deposit. My friend Bob suggested we write to a trust to try and get the deposit. If he can help us move away he will be giving four children a chance in life.

It ended in disappointment. We discovered that the rents are above what we would get from housing benefit. The landlords do not want people like me.

**5 March 1997**

This is the first time I have been able to write since my brother Joe died. He was my favourite brother and I was his favourite sister. It is so very hard for me to accept that I won't see him again. I have been just blanking it out of my mind. It is at times like this when you lose a loved one that I get angry with God and ask myself why does he take a young man who has two lovely children, a father, six brothers and eight sisters, and put us all in pain? My brother had a drink problem which started when he parted from his wife, and I know he was hurting very much inside. He felt nobody wanted him and just let himself go. I know he is happy now and in a far better place. He was not happy in this world and was very, very lonely. Maybe that is why God took him because he was suffering so much pain and heartache and did not know who to turn to for help. His children are a credit to him. I will stop now as I am getting emotional.

So much has happened in the past seven months. My son Peter has a drug habit, and one night I was along at the phone and as I was coming back I saw an ambulance at my door. I didn't think for a minute that it was for Peter. I was scared to go into the house but I eventually did and I ran upstairs to where the paramedics were trying to bring my son back – he had overdosed. I thank God that these people were there on time as the police told me that if he had been left for another couple of minutes I would have lost him. I am terrified every time he takes his poison – heroin. I have to keep shouting up to him to make sure he is still all right. I know Peter wants help and he has told me that this place, Easterhouse, is just making him worse. If I could move house to a different environment, I know he will come off this horrible stuff with the help of my doctor.

Easterhouse is just terrible. It is full of poverty, crime and drugs. I fear for the rest of my children as there is nothing here for them. If I stay here any longer then Morris, who is now twelve, and Maureen, nine, may fall into the evil ways. I am planning to go down to Royston beside my father. I know that drugs are all over but it is not as bad as here.

Angie, who is now fifteen, decided that she wanted to go into care rather than stay in Easterhouse. She is now in Cardross Children's Home until I get a move. It is heartbreaking that I have to put my child into care because of the environment we live in but I am glad she is away from here. She gets home at weekends to stay at my other daughter's in Yorkhill and she comes to stay with me one night a week.

Morris is very unhappy. He is at secondary school but he does not want to go to school or stay in Easterhouse any more. He was getting bullied by older boys and they were making him go with them to steal. It is so bad that I am now losing my children one by one.

I am determined to get away because if not Morris will end up in prison or on drugs. My other son, Bill, is now seventeen and has been lucky thanks to Bob, who took him under his wing when Bill was eight. I thank God that Bill knows all the dangers of drugs. He sees his big brother going through hell and vowed he would never try anything.

My children are all I have and I love them dearly, and that is why I have got to move from here to give them a future.

## 13 July 1997

I have not been writing for some time now. It is very hard for me just now, and I don't know where to begin as so many things have happened since I moved house. I am now in Royston having moved here in February. We are three floors up and the flat is a lot better than the one we had in Easterhouse. I was brought up in Royston, although it has all changed. Maureen is quite content but she is not the same happy wee girl she used to be. Morris is to go to a residential school, not because he has been bad or in trouble but because he missed so much schooling. The new school will give him all the support he needs, he will be at school every day and his emotional needs will be met. I will miss him terribly, but he will be coming home every weekend.

I don't think I am a bad person or done anything really

bad in this life, and neither has any of my family. So why is God punishing me? My brother Joe died and now my young brother George, who is in Nottingham, has been told he has cancer of the lungs. If anything happens to George, who is only thirty-five years old, I could not cope with it because I don't want to experience the pain and sorrow of losing another brother. Why does God let us suffer like this, even little children, as my wee Maureen broke her heart as she had been Uncle Joe's favourite? Please God help George, he is just a boy with all his life in front of him and three beautiful children.

Why, why, why, this family? I have suffered enough and don't want to go on any longer. I am worried about my kids. The past five weeks I have not been out of the house. I don't want to get up out of bed in the morning since I heard about George. When I do get up, I don't wash, I just sit in the chair thinking. I used to take great pride in my appearance, but I don't care now. My father lives just across the road with my young brother Albert. I have not been over to see my dad and he will be wondering what is wrong with me. I can't tell him as he does not know about George being ill. I feel as if I have just given up. If Albert knew how I am feeling I know he would understand and let my dad know I am depressed.

It is now 3 p.m. and I am feeling better because I have some good news. My daughter, Cheryl, is an air hostess with Virgin Airlines and she got her wings from Richard Branson. She is determined to make something of herself and is saving to get me and her brothers and sisters a new house. I am so very proud of her because she has made my dreams come true because I used to dream about being an air hostess. She has done it and I must be the proudest mam in the world. I am sure I will be just as proud of my other kids.

I am stopping now as I am going to phone my brother, Gerald, to find out how things are with George. Then I will phone Bob as I have got to talk to somebody about my brother as it is all building up inside me.

# Denise

I was born in 1974 so I am now twenty-two. We lived in Ballieston in Glasgow. I had three brothers and a sister, Pat. I was the youngest. I can't really remember my dad then. He moved to Oban, where he lived in a caravan, and I didn't really meet him until I was eleven. My mum was good to us.

When I was seven we moved to Easterhouse, to Duntarvie Quadrant. We had a lot of trouble with a family there, they terrified us, kicking in the door. They kicked the door in, came in, everybody screaming and shouting. They were not after me, it was a feud with my brothers. Afterwards we had to barricade the door. Once they sent an undertaker to us and we had to explain that no one had died. Then they poisoned our dog and it died. After that, I was about eleven, we moved to Corpach Place.

I did not like school. I started going around with my big brother buzzing glue, breaking into houses. I went to St Clare's School for a bit, which was better. Then I moved up to secondary school at St Leonard's, but I was not there long. One night we were out with our mum and she was steaming at two in the morning. She put out her hand to stop a taxi and just fell down. It wasn't a taxi, it was the police, and they picked us up and we were taken into care. We were told it would be for just one night, but it was three months. We went to Inver House, which is in the Commonhead part of Easterhouse. It was brilliant. You could do what you wanted. If you needed anything they got it for you. I was getting home to my mum at weekends and then I got back to her.

After that I kept running away. I couldn't put up with my mother drinking. I used to run out in my nightdress. I was taken back into care. I went to Inver House for a couple of months and then they moved me to Garfield. It was all right, the staff were nice. My mum used to come to see us and we went home sometimes. After a while, I wanted to go home again. I didn't like moving between the places and my mum had stopped drinking so I was home for my twelfth birthday. My dad came through from Oban. But he only stayed for a couple of months, just when I was getting to know him. I loved him. He has passed away now, about a year ago. Then mum started drinking again and it was back to Garfield for a good few months and then I was sent to the Good Shepherd Centre. While I was there my mum moved. She left me and went to Oban. I wasn't allowed to see her.

After a while, my big brother took me in for weekends. He stayed near the Highlands. But his girlfriend didn't want me. She was a snob and said I'd be trouble. In the end she was right as I messed that up and was back at the Good Shepherd. One of the nuns said she'd take me to see my mum. She took me but I had to sit in the social work office, I was not allowed to leave it, it was called a supervised visit. After I had seen mum, I'd walk about with the staff and get dinner before the four hour journey back. I got to go every couple of months. At first I was angry with my mum, then I was angry with the staff because they would not let me be with my mum and the rest of my family. I just wanted to get back to the time when my mum was not drinking.

Mum was staying in a caravan in Oban, so I used to run away and make my own way up. I used to get on a train and hide in the toilet. Mum used to say, 'What are you doing up here on your own?' But she would keep me there, she would not phone the police and she hid me from them. They found me in the toilet, in the shower bit, and they took me back.

As soon as I got back to the Good Shepherd, I absconded again. This time I went with some of my pals to Paisley. We tried to break into a shop and hid in the bins at the back. The police came and caught a few of them but me and another pal never got caught. Later I was terrified staying out on the streets all night. I was still young, about thirteen. We slept in a cul-de-sac and I was wishing that I had been caught by the police and taken back. After that we went to Glasgow, walked about town, met up with other people in gangs, the Celtic Casuals. We used to hang about with them and go to the alleys where there are heaters coming up through the grills in the ground and we slept there. We were shoplifting for food and taking clothes off washing lines. Then the boys did a break-in, we were standing to take the stuff and we were caught by the police. We were taken back to the home.

Because I had kept running away, I was not allowed to see my mother and brothers in Oban. But after a couple of years, they started taking me up again and then they allowed me to go on my own. I had to go to a school inside the Good Shepherd as they thought I might run away if I went to a school outside. I could not get on in school. I used to fight in class and jump through the window. I can't cope in a crowd. Then I was sent to a special school with only six in a class. I found it great. The school was in Glasgow so I got sent back to Inver House in Easterhouse. As I was now going to school, I was allowed to spend weekends with my sister, Pat, who by this time was living in Auchencrow Street in Easterhouse. It went great and it ended up with us going to a children's panel and I was allowed to go and live with Pat. I didn't like her boyfriend and I used to go out and get drunk and fight with them. Then he caught me buzzing gas in front of the gas fire and he gave me a doing so I said I wanted to go back into care. I went back to Inver House, I was fifteen.

After a while, I was allowed back to my sister. I kept out of trouble, except for a bit of drink, and I went to school until I left at 16. I went up to Oban for a night out with a pal and there I met Colin. The next day I came back to Glasgow and a few days later Colin turns up with my big brother. My sister said he could stay a couple of days but he ended up staying altogether.

I went on a training course and they sent us on a kind of job. But I had a fight and got kicked out first day. I was pregnant and we got a flat at 8, Dalswinton Street. Our baby, Sally, was born a month before my seventeenth birthday. I used to take the baby to see my mum in Oban sometimes. Once I went to Oban and left Sally with my pal. My sister did not think this was right and took Sally off her. The social workers got involved and warned me that if it happened again, they would ask for a supervision order on the baby.

We were in 8, Dalswinton Street for eight months and were then moved to 17, Lochdochart Road. We had to start from scratch because our house had got broken into in Dalswinton Street. We had a bed and that was it. Captain Buchanan at the Salvation Army helped us get more furniture. When I was nineteen, I fell pregnant again and Chris was born. We stayed in the house all the time except for an odd visit to bingo. My sister used to look after the children now and then, but then she moved to Oban. When I was twenty, we had the third baby, Wally. We can't go out and leave the babies with anybody in case the social workers take them off us.

The tenement was knocked down so we moved to 19, Dalswinton Street. We didn't even have a carpet. One day our wee boy climbed on his bike to put the light on and fell on the bare floorboards and had a bruise under his eye. I had gone out to the van to buy some food and had asked a fifteen-year-old lassie to keep an eye on them. The next day the health visitor called and asked me about the bruise. I said, 'Are you saying I am beating up my wean? Do you want to see his body?' She said no, but I stripped him and she said 'That's fine.' But she phoned the social workers. They came to the door and told me that they had heard from the health visitor that my boy had a bruise. I said, 'That's right' and showed them the bare boards where he fell. At the end, the social worker said the kids were well looked after. She told me to come to the office next day to see if it was to be taken further. I went the next morning and it was all right.

I am stuck in most of the time. We get up and I make breakfast. Colin is brilliant with the kids and he takes Sally to school. And he does the housework. We make lunch and then take Chris to nursery. Then we collect them from school and nursery and get dinner. We wash them and put them to bed about seven o'clock. Then we sit on the bed and watch telly which saves putting the fire on. Occasionally we go to bingo. We can't go outside the door at night because there are junkies' needles lying about. They thought I was selling drugs and the police kicked in our door and searched the flat. But there is nothing. We have smoked a little drop of hash and that is all.

I just live off my giro book. We get £120 a fortnight but it is a £100 now because I have a social fund loan. Then I get child benefit on Wednesdays. As soon as I get paid, I buy food and some sweets for the kids to take to school. Then I pay the catalogue £40 a fortnight. With the child benefit, I buy powercards for the electricity. I can't remember having new clothes for myself. My sister hands me on some of hers. At times I do get really fed up and think I can't be bothered. Then I might have a bath and go to bed for a wee greet[3] to myself. We've got each other and we've been together six years.

In the future when the weans are grown up, I'd like to have a job so I can get out of the house. I'd like to work in a hospital. I'd like to move somewhere quiet.

# Penny

I was born in Easterhouse, Glasgow, where my parents had lived for a good few years, and lived in Glassel Road. I remember the first day I started school at St Clare's. I was very smart and I really enjoyed it. I had plenty of friends and enjoyed my childhood. But my father was really strict, and if he told us to be in at a certain time and we were late he would beat us.

My mum fell pregnant and we moved to Garthamlock, which is a part of Greater Easterhouse. I was about eleven when we moved and I remember starting at high school, at St Gregory's, which I enjoyed. I used to like going on day trips with my parents and friends. My father was out of work a lot and used to go to the pubs. When he returned he would argue with my mum. There was a crucifix on the wall, and I remember him taking it down and splitting my mother's head open and she had twenty-eight stitches. I knew that my mother loved me, but my father was always more for his sons and I found it difficult to speak to him.

When I was fifteen, the teacher told me that I would be able to leave school. I could not sign on for unemployment and I had no money so I felt fed up. My mum asked me to go into work with her to give her a hand cleaning in a chip shop in Glasgow. I liked that, and one day the boss asked me to work for him. It was great and I was able to give money to my parents to help out in the house because my parents had four children. But then the boss sold the shop so me and my mum were out of work. I was just sixteen and my father told me I would have to go and look for another job.

I went to the Job Centre where the woman sent me for an interview at the Cereal Mill in Washington Street where I got a job packing lentils. I enjoyed it because I made some good friends. Sometimes we used to go dancing or for a drink at the weekends. I was there for about three years, but then a number of us got paid off.

By this time I was eighteen and out of work. I had been seeing a young man called Terry for a long time. Then we split up because we were not getting on. But then I found out I was pregnant. I told Terry and he didn't want to know. He told me that he was too young to be tied down with a family. I was young, out of work, still living with my parents and about to have a baby. When my parents found out I was expecting, my father was really angry and said he did not want a bastard in his house but my mum was OK. I was taken into Rotten Row Hospital and a doctor spoke to me about having a termination. I was determined not to do that and that I would bring the baby up even on my own. When the baby was born my father came to see me and said he was sorry for what he had said. My parents decided that they would help to bring up the child and that was a great help. I was nineteen when I had a lovely baby boy, I called him Alistair. His father never got in touch with me, never even sent Alistair a birthday card or Christmas card.

So I just got on with life with my son until I had a

bust-up with my parents. My father got fed up with Alistair crying. If I wanted to go out, I had to ask my mother to babysit, and my father did not like that and said that if I had decided to have a baby I should bring it up. So I left home. I had no one to turn to. One brother was in the army, the other was too young. I ended up in the council's homeless unit. We were there for seven months. It was tough. Alistair was a few months old and the hostel was cold. It was only bed and breakfast, so you had to stay out for your lunch and tea. I walked about looking in shops. Sometimes I felt like taking my own life, but I had to think of my son. I wrote to Alistair's dad and asked him if he would help because of my circumstances but he was not interested.

Then I got housed back in Easterhouse, in Easterhouse Quad, where I stayed for a couple of years with my son. The flat was OK and some of the neighbours were nice, but others did not like me because I was a Catholic. When one family had been out drinking, they would shout through my letterbox, 'You're a Fenian bastard.' I could not take it any more and I complained to the council. But in the end I had to move myself and I moved in with a girlfriend for a while before the council offered me a place in Duntarvie Road. I was there for a couple of years but had to move again because the council was taking off the top storeys of the flats. I was re-housed in Kildermorie Road.

By this time I had met up with John. He had asked me out for a drink. He moved in with me and we got on well together and he got on with my son. It was great. I fell pregnant with John's baby and Mandy was born. Then everything started going wrong. I caught him taking drugs, he had a syringe sticking in his arm − heroin. I found out John had been taking drugs and when I asked him about it, he told me to shut my mouth. One day I found the home smelling with glue which John and a friend had been sniffing. I was so shocked that I phoned the Social Work Department and they came with the police and put John out of the house. The next day John came back and said he was sorry, so I forgave him and we got back together again. Then I got pregnant again and had another daughter, Kim. By this time John was bringing drugs into the house. I was going out of my head with worry. I was so fed up that I ran away with the kids to Manchester, where I had a brother. He didn't have the room to take us, so the police took us to the homeless unit and the council gave us tickets back to Glasgow. Back in Glasgow, the Housing Department refused to rehouse me as they said I had made myself intentionally homeless and that I would have to stay on the streets for a year. I went to stay with another girlfriend in Easterhouse. She had a boyfriend and a baby and it was only a two-bedroomed flat. Then John joined us. My friend got fed up with not having any privacy. I ended up going back into the homeless unit.

We were rehoused in Dalilea Drive, Easterhouse. It was here I met Captain Buchanan of the Salvation Army. I remember him telling me to get rid of John and saying I would not have a good life with him. Alistair, who was then about nine, started going to the clubs at the Salvation Army, and Bob took him to the camps with the Covenanters.

I was moved to another housing scheme, Queenslie, which is also a part of Greater Easterhouse. John was there, but I hardly saw him as he was too busy away taking drugs, I did not stay in the house for all that long because something happened to one of my daughters. I asked a neighbour to watch the two girls while I went to the shops. When I got back my oldest daughter was very upset. She went into the toilet and started screaming. She was saturated with blood. She told me that one of the neighbours had put himself on top of her and done something down below. He then threatened her with a knife. I called the police. They took me and Mandy to the police station and we were there for hours with two CID women and they took her to Yorkhill Hospital and the police surgeon said she had been sexually assaulted. We did not get home until 4.30 in the morning. Later that morning I was told that if I did not move out of Queenslie our place would get petrol-bombed. I phoned the police and they came out. I phoned the Social Work Department and they put us in the homeless unit. The police took the man to the police station and the forensic people said there was a hair in Mandy's clothing from his head. They said it was his word against hers and, as there were no witnesses, he was not prosecuted. But Mandy had to have sixteen sessions of counselling, and the counsellor said she had been sexually abused. I heard later that some of the Queenslie boys went and set his place on fire after they heard what had happened.

So we were all put back into the homeless unit. It was terrible, I felt so sorry for my three children. They didn't know if they were coming or going. They put me and

John and the children into just one basement room with one double bed, three single beds, a fire with just one bar. I was always telling the children to keep the noise down. They had to change schools again. We had to be out for other meals, eating bags of chips, sitting in laundrettes. Alistair started being cheeky to me and running away. I felt I could not control him. He seemed to blame me for all the moves and I knew that deep inside he just wanted to settle down. The Housing Department were saying that we should not have moved out of Queenslie and that the bloke who abused Mandy should have gone. In the end Bob phoned up the chief man in the housing and then wrote a letter to the paper and we got rehoused. It was just after Xmas that the Housing Department decided to rehouse me and my partner back in Easterhouse. I went to Dalswinton Street in Rogerfield. I loved the house, and it was handy for the school, which was just across the road. It was also near the Salvation Army, so Alistair could go to the clubs again. He loved the clubs and it got him out of the house. He won a trophy for darts, he was over the moon about that and I was really proud of him. He went to camp and to a holiday at Millport. I started going to the Salvation Army. I got on great with Captain Buchanan and I enjoyed meeting different people.

Me and my family settled down until my partner started on the drugs again. He had promised that he had stopped but things really got out of hand. Every day he would bring someone in taking drugs. He would even sell things from the house for drugs. If I told him to stop, he would tell me to shut up. He would take the kids' food money to buy drugs. I reported it to social workers and they told John he should get help, but he would deny that he had a problem. I went to see our GP and she put him on temgezics and told him not to inject. He did that for two days and then he was selling the temgezics to get heroin. I had to ask for clothes and food from the Social Work Department and the Salvation Army. I used to get embarrassed about asking. It was that bad that social workers took us to a children's panel, but nothing happened. I had no life with John but he told me that if I left him he would take the two girls from me. The girls did love their dad. So I stayed with John for the sake of his kids. Alistair never liked John because of what he was doing to me, taking money from me, stealing, taking drugs. This made him play up.

One Saturday night I was sitting in the house with my three children. My mother was also there visiting us. Suddenly the police came to my door and told me that John was in hospital. He had been attacked outside the shops and slashed with broken bottles and had nineteen wounds. I was told it was from people who he had not paid for drugs. On the Sunday morning, men broke into my kids' bedroom and set the house on fire. My children were terrified. I ran to Bob's and we phoned the fire and police. The police said it was because of what had happened to John. He had told them the names of the men who had attacked him and it was a threat that he should not grass. The police said it wasn't safe for us in Rogerfield, so once again we were in the homeless unit. Me and John and the kids were in bed and breakfast for a while.

By this time, I had had enough of moving from hostels to houses, I just wanted to settle down with the children. Then I got a letter from the council offering us a place in another part of Glasgow. I said to myself, this is the end, and I swore I was not going to move any more through John and drugs. I had been there about four months and it was a Monday night. I was again sitting with the three children and my mother. Then a couple of men came to the door looking for John. They pulled out knives and said they were going to kill John because he was a grass. John was out, away buying more drugs. When he came home my mother told him and he phoned the police. The police said it was best if we left and we went back to the homeless unit. Once more we went to bed and breakfast. Apart from breakfast we had to stay out. It was terrible, especially for the children. I just couldn't take any more. A couple of weeks before Christmas, we were moved right away from Glasgow to another town. It was another change of school for Alistair, who was just about to start at secondary school, and Mandy.

The house was great and some of the neighbours were all right. But John was still taking drugs. I even went to see a drugs counsellor about him. Then I went to see my GP about him, but she said that if John wanted help to come off drugs then he would have to go and see her himself. Then, with John injecting drugs into his groin, his main artery burst, he lost seven pints of blood, and he ended up on a life support machine. He stayed in hospital for twelve weeks and I took the children to see him every day. While he was there, John started receiving treatment for his drugs. One of the doctors told him that if he went back to drugs he would kill himself. While John was in hospital, my house was broken into by the junkies that stayed in our close.

Things were all right when John got out of hospital, but he had to walk with a walking stick, so the stairs in the close were too much for him. The council gave us another house. As there were no vacancies on ground floors, we were moved to a village. Then John started drinking and drinking heavily. If I didn't give him money for drink he would beat me up. I was so frightened. He came home so drunk that he threw me and the kids out on the street. Then my son Alistair started hanging around with a boy called Tony. My partner got to know Tony's parents and used to go over to their house to drink with them. He would come home drunk during the night and would shout and swear and beat me up. Then he would turn the music up full blast and wake the kids and wake the neighbours. It was terrible. I thought about leaving but I had nowhere to go. My parents were getting on and if I had gone to them they could not have put up with all the hassle from John.

Social workers were coming in and out of the house all the time because of all the carry on. I just didn't know which way to turn. I was going round and round in my head, trying to work things out and trying to get the family back to normal. But things just got worse with John bringing all sorts of people into the house. I felt the home was not mine any more and that I had no say in the matter.

One night, John brought Tony's parents into the house to drink. They got very drunk and John fell asleep in the

chair, so I asked Tony's parents to leave. When John woke
he beat me up for asking his drinking friends to go. Plus
John also beat up Alistair and smashed his glasses into his
face and he attacked a neighbour. The police came and he
was taken away and charged with two assaults but the
court let him off. Alistair told the social workers he did
not want to stay in the same house as John and they went
to the Sheriff's Court for a warrant to take him away.
Later he went to a children's panel and the members told
me that they were taking Alistair into care for his own
safety.

It was in 1995 that Alistair went into care and he has
been there ever since. He hates John for what he has done
to me and his sisters. He says he will never forget or
forgive him. But I still stayed in the house with John and
our daughters.

John then started staying out of the house. He spent
more time drinking with his friends than with his
children. He even got barred from the local pubs for
fighting and begging. John always had to have money, the
world had to be around him. If it was not drugs, it was
drink. He has a big problem and he should get help.

I have put up with violence, drugs and drinking
problems. I knew that I was going to leave John because
me and the kids have been through a lot and we could
not put up with this torture. Finally one Tuesday, John
went to collect our money and all he handed me was
£20 to buy food, coal and clothes for four of us. I told
him I wanted the rest. John then left and went to his
brother's. I packed our clothes and me and the children
left the house. I went to the social workers and told them

what had happened. My social worker phoned Women's Aid but they were fully booked so we had to go into the homeless unit. This was in March 1996.

John found out we were in the homeless unit and he came and threatened the caretaker and fought people there. I then decided to go back to John because he told me he was going to change and that he was going to be a better father to his children. He was off the drink for a couple of weeks. My social worker got me a holiday at Wonderwest with the kids so as to give us a break. But when I got back the social workers started calling every day to make sure that John never started his carry-on. I began to see that John had never changed and that time was running out.

I decided to leave John for good. We went back to the homeless unit, but John started harassing the people there again. The caretaker phoned the police and he was charged. I went on staying in the hostel and I never went back to John. We were in the hostel for two months and then the Housing Department got me a house. The social workers helped me get items for it. It was great not having to live with someone that takes drugs and comes in drunk. It is bliss. I have my own money and my two kids have settled down at a new school, have made new friends and are very happy. I am my own boss and do what I want to do. I still see my son Alistair, who is now sixteen, and he says I should have left John years ago. The only reason I never left John was because of the girls. But when I look back and think of all the violence and the beatings, John stealing from me, all the times I have had to move, it makes me feel sick. My oldest girl is nearly eleven and my youngest daughter is nearly eight. This is a new start and I want to get on with my life and give my daughters the life they never had. May the rest of our lives be happy ones.

## 1997

I am writing again. John found us and we were moved again to a village. It was great. My son Alistair came home at last and I decorated the house really well. My daughters liked the school and Mandy went to the Sunday School and a club at the church. Alistair had been in foster homes which did not work out, and then he went to a hostel and came to see us at weekends. He had a job for a bit. Then he started bringing the wrong kind of people to the house and caused commotions so I had to stop it. He started stealing cars. He went to Glasgow to stay with my brother, where he started drinking. Then they drove in a car, did not pay for the petrol, they were chased by the police and crashed. Alistair was sent to a Young Offenders Institution for three months and put on two years' probation and banned from driving for three years. It was in the local paper so I was the talk of the village. Alistair started sending letters saying he wanted to see me. How could I manage to visit? In the end, I got people to run me over but I had to pay them £12. It was a terrible-looking place. He was in the health centre there as he was considered a danger to himself. He asked me for money for stamps and his soap. I gave him some money and when I got back I went to the DSS for a crisis loan and they refused. I phoned the Social Work Department and they brought me some food.

I get only £62 a week income support plus £19.60 child benefit. From that I have to pay food, the council tax, powercards, stamps for the TV, a card for the light meter. I used to get £76, but it was cut because I had a loan for bedding. I asked for another loan for some clothes for my daughters but they would not give it. Then I asked for a loan as I do not have a washing machine. I was turned down again. I appealed but it failed. You used to get grants for things like that. I find it very hard to live on the money I get. For the kids' clothes, I go to the charity shops, I cannot afford to go into a proper shop like Poundstretchers or British Home Stores. The government keep telling you to claim for this and that, yet when you claim you are refused. It is not right. I find it really hard to live on benefits and I feel sorry for other people who are struggling too. But I do manage and I do not have to go and borrow from neighbours.

In some ways I was doing well. The social worker said it was marvellous how I managed the money. Mandy and Kim had been put on the 'at risk' register because of John and under supervision, and now they were taken off. But then it all went bad again.

Just before Christmas 1996, my doorbell went. It was John. He pushed his way in, he was drunk and assaulted me. I got the police and there was a fight, with him shouting and bawling. The street where I stay is all old folk and they complained to the council. Two months later, John came again, drunk again, and broke into one of my neighbours' homes. They complained to the council and the Housing told me it would have to stop. I told John not to come but he would not listen. One night he hammered on the door at eleven o'clock. He was covered in blood and was in a taxi without any money and the driver wanted £3 from me. I told the taxi man to phone the police as he did not stay with me. The police came and took John away and charged him with fraud. It was terrible. Two weeks later he was caught stealing from my local shop and he went to prison for a short while. Again people complained to the council and then signed a petition to get me put out of my house. They even said that I left my kids in the street until all hours in the night. I was unhappy with the neighbours and worried sick. In June, I was served a Notice of Proceedings for recovery of possession of the dwelling and the housing officer told me, in front of my children, I had no chance of being rehoused by the council. She told me she would write to Manchester to see if they would take me as I have a brother who lives there. I am now on Valium tablets and under the hospital where I see a psychiatrist as I am suffering from what is called post-trauma stress. I hope this will get me rehoused.

I went to a meeting called a Network Meeting with my solicitor and with a lawyer to speak for me with the Housing Department. The housing people said John had been living in my home, which was all lies. They said I was being referred to Manchester.

# Cynthia

Plant Street in Denistoun was typical of inner-city housing in the Fifties. Run-down tenement flats with outside, shared toilets, open back courts and lots of large families crammed into small rooms.

Word was spreading like wildfire that the corporation were building wonderful new houses way out in the countryside in places called schemes. Could it be true? Could we get one? Amazingly the answer to both questions was yes! We could get one and it would be ready for us in March 1960. I was only a baby so I stayed with mum and Jane who was three while dad took Ingrid, six, and Alice, seven, on the 22 bus to Easterhouse.

Dad loved living in the city, it was where he was brought up, where his people lived and where he felt he belonged. Plant Street was no worse than any other, and although he was the first to admit we were overcrowded at least he had an all-girl family so that didn't really matter. Anyway he always 'had a few wee deals going'. What could he do stuck out in the middle of nowhere? My da also enjoyed a pint (and a half) and he'd heard there were NO pubs in Easterhouse, so that was added to his long list of reasons for not to go and live there. Mum had just as many reasons not to stay in Plant Street. She was sick of living in a room and a kitchen, of sharing toilets that were dirty and never seemed to work, and all the neighbours had either sold up and left or were planning to go very soon.

My da changed his mind on that first day, but not because of anything mum said. He changed his mind when he saw the fields and country roads. My gran was born on the Isle of Arran and he had spent many happy times there and had loved to take long walks ever since. This scheme idea might not be so bad after all. What clinched it was the garden, it was huge. We had been offered a corner house, bottom flat in a close with only six flats. He pictured the garden with trees and paths and flower beds, even stairs AND we would have a veranda, he would put a gate in that and get straight to the garden from the living room!

Mum was delighted. She couldn't believe we had a living room, separate kitchen, two bedrooms AND that indoor toilet with a bath! Three years later we had another sister, confirming dad's belief that he worked all his days to buy knickers! So there we were, five girls, mum, dad and the pets. Our pets were the talk of the place. We had the usual succession of dogs but also a few that were a bit more unusual.

Chip was one of the best. She would beg and jump up quite a height for tit-bits. She came when we called her name and loved being scratched under her chin. She also paid for her board by providing breakfast every day because Chip was a chicken! We kept Chip in a large hutch in the garden, which by now had all the paths and stairs dad had dreamed of on that first day. It also had a heart-shaped pond that became a flower bed when dad got fed up clearing out the bread we insisted on putting in to feed the fish. Chip had the run of the whole garden and attracted quite a bit of attention. Sometimes she wandered out through a space in the hedge but that wasn't a problem as we also had Chas.

Chas was the next best thing to a sheepdog, a wee mongrel that could round up anything. We only had to shout, 'Find Chip' and he'd run along Canonbie Street barking like mad and he always found her.

Over the years we had many pets in that hutch, including rabbits and guinea pigs. For a while we even had two ducks, but no matter what it was Chas would round them up. He was very gentle with all of them and brought them all back except other dogs. Dad was a well-known animal lover so we always ended up with everyone else's unwanted pets or injured birds. I've lost count of all the animals that shared our garden, veranda and even the house, but while we had Chas no other dog stayed long. They got through the hedge, followed him past the bus terminus and were never seen again!

Chas was trouble, he would wander over to a group of dogs all of whom were quite happy, snap at a few heels, get a good fight going and wander back to the garden the picture of innocence leaving behind a rabble of snarling dogs and raging owners. It was while running back from one such fight that he was hit by a car. He broke his leg and was quiet for a while, which was good for the neighbours but bad for us as we had to round up Chip ourselves.

Snap was another dog we had for years. He was a golden Labrador and he was gorgeous. I used to sit for hours scooping marrow from bones and feeding it to him with a spoon. I'd brush his coat and play with him all day but still he seemed to prefer my wee sister Ruth. He stayed beside her all the time and walked between her and anyone else. I told her he only protected her because I told him to, that made me feel a bit better.

At this time, dad was a lorry driver and we always knew when he was coming home as Snap would bark to get into the garden long before the lorry appeared in the street. Snap was stolen from us, and although we couldn't prove it we knew who had taken him. They gave him away and we never saw him again and to this day I still hold it against them.

We also had birds, Peking robins. We started off with two but ended up with lots of them. They were nice to look at but I've always hated birds flying about. I'm frightened of them and was quite happy when we gave them all away. We didn't really have any choice, they are attracted to light and we had a coal fire, the daft birds kept flying towards it and after a nasty accident when the fire guard was left off we thought they should go.

Easterhouse was built in a hurry and was a big mistake. I don't know when I first realized that but it wasn't when I was happily playing with my family and our pets in Lochdochart Road. For me Easterhouse was fun, friendly and home. I went to Bishoploch School, played kick-the-can and rounders and went for long, long walks with my dad through the miles of countryside right on our doorstep. We jumped the burns in the peat fields where Commonhead stands now and walked to Drumpellier twice a day during the school holidays when it was only a loch with an old boating shed and toilets that were so dirty everyone preferred to go in the bushes. We didn't need our parents to come with us, it was safe to stay away all day and we only came home when it got dark or we got hungry.

Hogganfield Loch was another favourite walk for us. Again I went here both with my dad and with friends. It's further away, but at that time Craigend wasn't in the way so we could walk over the fields. Hogganfield had lots of small hills you can run down, and jump in front of your dad on the path at the bottom. It was good fun, at least it was till my young sister tried it, tripped over the kerb and burst her nose open! That put an end to the game and gave me serious doubts about my dad's decision-making. After all it was him who insisted she could come walks in the first place.

If I needed any further proof that he was wrong it came very soon. We went round Bishops Loch. This was a favourite walk for us, there were sandy pits every now and then and we'd stop at each one to play and dad would make a roll-up, sit down and enjoy his wee smoke. He'd tell us all about Gartcosh Hospital and how it used to be a big house with all these grounds and a home farm with orchards and everything.

It was a very impressive place and could easily be again with some imagination and some investment, but at that time we loved it and it was just fun to be there. On this particular day my uncle Jim and his two boys were with us (me, dad, Jane and Ruth). We kids were running ahead as usual and were jumping 'the burns'. These were actually outlets from the hospital sewers and were badly contaminated, but we didn't know that and there had never been a problem. Then Ruth fell in. Uncle Jim got to her first and managed to get her out. Later I realized how serious it had been and how ill she was, but at the time it just proved my point that she should stay at home, and another great game was ruined. AND we all walked home in our vests because she had our jumpers on, see what I mean?

There was another game she managed to put the damper on but didn't quite spoil. Rafting in the quarry pit in the peat fields. A crowd of us played there, and although we stayed away from the huge hills of gravel and sand we just couldn't understand why Ruth (and our parents) were worried about us making a perfectly good raft from a pallet and sailing over our 'lake'. We used to pretend we were stuck in the middle, but Ruth cried and shouted so much we had to stop just in case the watchie heard her and chased us home. She may not have been as adventurous as us but she never told our mums so she was all right really.

I went to Bishoploch Primary School and a few of my friends went to St Clare's. This didn't cause any friction or problems, just as it causes no problems now for my own kids and their friends. But then and now the trouble always erupts between Lochend and St Leonard's, the secondary schools. I don't believe this is a religious thing at all, it's more of a tradition. The two schools are directly facing each other, and for a lot of the boys in my classes it seemed natural to 'fight the Lenny'.

With so many cutbacks in education and so many schools closing through lack of money and falling rolls, I sometimes wonder if the answer might lie in demolishing the two schools and replacing them with ONE modern mixed school with better facilities for the whole community. This idea would have horrified my dad as he was an Orangeman all his life and would never have agreed to his girls going to a Catholic school. But times change and sometimes we have to change with them or be left at the bottom of some pen-pusher's list of priorities.

I liked dad being in the Orange Lodge, I even joined myself for a while. It was fun. We went to meetings and parties and marched behind the band. I didn't connect it to Ireland and the fighting over there, but slowly over the years I discovered the more serious side to it and decided it wasn't for me after all. I'm sure my dad was very disappointed, but he didn't really show it and only said it was my decision. Even us being in the Lodge didn't cause any fighting amongst our neighbours. As I said, religion didn't come into it, and yet there were gang fights in Easterhouse just as there is now and again, it's almost like a tradition.

Easterhouse has always been as big as a town but has never been recognized as one. Therefore it's never had the facilities it needs to behave like a town with an identifiable centre and surrounding districts. Despite this lack of planning it has become very parochial and that is where the gang fighting comes in. We lived in Drummy and our gang was called 'The Drummy'. Rogerfield, being on the other side of the pitches, were the natural enemy and they had 'The Aggro'. The other big gang was 'The Toi', which later became 'The Torran Toi'. There were plenty of fights, some of them very serious, but it really didn't affect us very much. We heard about them and sometimes we heard them running back from the pitches but we didn't have any boys in our family till my brother was born in 1970, and we left Drummy in 1977 so he never got involved.

Everyone called the Lochend area Drummy or Drummyland. We even had dances in the church called Drummy Dances. There was very little trouble at them, but some of the people from Liff Place complained about the noise and they eventually stopped having them and everyone had to go to the Project dances instead. That was the entertainment. If you wanted to go swimming you went to Townhead or Shettleston and if you wanted anything else you went somewhere else.

The lack of facilities in Easterhouse today is a scandal, but thirty years ago things were even worse. When my mum went shopping she HAD to go either into town or to Duke Street or the Gallowgate as we only had very small local shops that were too expensive for a weekly shop for a family with five kids and only one breadwinner. My elder sisters had to travel to schools in Dennistoun and we never heard of a community centre, never mind a sports complex.

When the planners and councillors moved us all out here they used the tenement model that worked well in the city, but they ignored the fact that it only worked so well elsewhere because everything else you needed was included in the design. The ground floor was used for shops and pubs. Doctors and dentists were local. Schools were local, and you only caught a bus if you wanted to visit someone or go into the city centre. This caused a lot of problems for the adults, but it seemed normal to me and I was quite happy as 'John the Vicky' our ice-cream van sold absolutely everything I needed to buy, and if I fancied a change and could afford it I could always wait for Mr Whippy.

We made our own entertainment, and every other week in the summer we'd put on a show. We all sang the same songs and did the same turns like 'I'm a little Dutch girl' and 'Lady of Spain', but we never tired of it and never considered it may be boring for the audience. We also played shops a lot, usually in the back courts with tin cans, dirt and grass for our goods and glass for money. When it rained we played in the closes as there were no security doors to get in the way. There was also no fences in the backs, so we could get from Lochdochart Road to Dalilea Drive in seconds. This made hide-and-seek a very long game and kick-the-can even longer.

The huge back courts were very busy places, especially during the school holidays. We had a big corner garden with part of it simply grassed over for us to play in, but the back was the place to be. During the day it was full of kids, but in the evening, when all the washings had been taken in and we had all been fed, was my favourite time. That's when a lot of our mums and sometimes our dads too would come out and play with us. We used the washing-line as play ropes, played balls against the gable end walls and best of all played endless games of rounders with about twenty in each team. They usually ended up a shambles with everyone arguing over who had won, but it was good fun. We also played a lot of games right over the road like 'farmer, farmer'. We didn't consider this dangerous and I can't remember anyone ever getting hurt. I suppose the few people who had cars and the bus drivers were used to us.

Our favourite pastime did cost money and was worth every penny, SCRAPS. We played with our scraps all the time. We bought them in strips and spent hours sorting them out into sets and putting them into books ready for swapping. Every scrap had either yes or no on the back to indicate whether or not you were willing to swap it. All the girls had scrap books and we knew exactly how many we had and which ones we were looking for. We never went inside each others' houses to swap, for some unknown reason we sat on the close stairs even in the winter. One unwritten rule was that you NEVER took anyone's scraps EVER, so it was inevitable that I had to fight with June Earl when she did the unforgivable and stole one of mine.

I had the usual arguments and slanging matches at school, but I was never a fighter. Even so, stealing scraps was the worst, so I set out to get June. I found her on her stairs and just flew for her. I pulled her hair right down as far as I could and seemed to be winning until she sunk her teeth into my leg! The pain was so bad I screamed blue murder, but she wouldn't let go. I was punching into her back and still screaming, and soon her mum came out along with all the other neighbours and they managed to prise her teeth open. I was in tears and my leg was sore for days, but I got my scrap back and her mum skelped[4] her and kept her in, so I didn't care too much (even when someone told my mum and I got kept in too).

Apart from buying scraps, money wasn't a big deal

when I was growing up because very few people had any. While I'm sure this caused a few headaches for our parents it seldom affected us. New clothes were quite rare, there was no shame in hand–me–downs. The only toys we really bothered with were dolls, and none of our friends went away on holiday, so we didn't feel we missed out.

We did however get new clothes every first Sunday in May. It would be a great shame for the whole family if you didn't. I always got a new dress, white socks and white sannies.[5] Most years our gran would knit us a new cardigan as well. We had to whiten the sannies at night and put them out on the windowsill to dry, and I always promised myself I'd keep them clean, but it's hard to remember daft promises when you're jumping burns!

Clothes didn't hold any interest for me until I went to secondary school, and by then I had the perfect solution to my problem. I knew I couldn't have the kind of gear I wanted, but Jane could because she was working. By this time my two eldest sisters had left home and Jane was doing piecework in a machinist factory in the town. This meant she was being paid according to how much work she produced so that meant lots of overtime. While she was at work I had full use of her wardrobe. I used to iron the stuff and have it back before she got home. She found out of course and she got really mad, but it was worth it and her threats never stopped me. Every now and then she still moans about it and tells me how annoying it was. But it wasn't my fault, she was older and out working first.

Although we didn't go on holidays we often went away

for the day, usually to Helensburgh. My dad would come in and shout, 'Who wants to go on the blue train?' and we'd all scream and rush about mad getting things ready. We always took a picnic with us, including the teapot which was put over the fire we always made on the beach. We played for hours in the water and on the sand and we always got chips to eat on the way home.

Sometimes we went to Portobello, but Ruth had an accident there too. She was running up from the water and a donkey stood on her toe! We had to wait for ages in the first aid hut and we came home afterwards, so it wasn't exactly our best day out. We didn't go on the train that day, we went in my dad's lorry. He'd been delivering to the fruit market and one of the men there had given him a big bag of strawberries for us, but I forgot they were on the seat and sat on them.

My dad drove articulated lorries for years and I loved it. He used to take me with him on his runs a lot, and we went to great places like Edinburgh and Aberdeen and the borders. He used to park the empty trailer outside our house, and it was a smashing place to play especially since we decided who was allowed on. One of my favourite runs was to a tent factory in Leith. The women there were really nice and always gave me sweets and bits of material, and after dad had finished unloading we'd go to the docks, then to the chippy. Dad always managed to get samples of whatever he was delivering, and while he seemed happiest when it was whisky or rum, I much preferred the cooking chocolate and condensed milk.

One sample he was sorry he brought home was a big load of cooking fat. He cooked some sausages in it and they tasted vile, so he put them on the coal fire to help light it, but it set fire to the chimney and bits fell out and burnt the carpet. All the neighbours were out watching the flames leaping from our chimney and dad was really embarrassed, more so when he found out the cooking fat was bound for a make-up factory and was not for human consumption.

One day not long after this dad pointed out a wee green van parked in the gable end between our close and the Williamsons. He said we should give it a wash. We did this very grudgingly as we didn't see why we should clean the Williamson's van when they had kids of their own. It wasn't until it was spotless that dad told us the van was ours, and as soon as we had our tea he took us for our first run. I can't describe how excited we were, it was like a dream. We went to the Campsies and played for a while, but all we wanted was to get back in the van. We sang all the way home and waved to all the other drivers out of the back window. We had other cars after that, some bangers, some not, but that wee green van was special.

We went lots of runs in the van, but Campsie Glen was our favourite. We'd paddle in the river and walk along the banks then race back up the big hill to the car park. During one of these races, mum lost her shoe and it was dark before we found it. We had a good laugh but she wasn't too chuffed and didn't race next time.

When I was about ten or eleven, we heard some very bad news. A new housing scheme (Commonhead) was to be built. How could we have any fun now? Commonhead was being put up on our peat fields, and the quarry was demolished. We soon discovered another source of fun, though... the building site. We spent many happy weeks playing in the huge pipes they brought in and even played on the new buildings and scaffolding now and then, but the watchie soon chased us from there. Better news was to come, because one of the people who moved into the new houses was to become my best friend for years. Her name was Joyce, and when she joined my class at Lochend we became inseparable.

Joyce lived with her mum and her young brother, her dad lived in Springburn with her older brother. We got on straight away and Joyce became like one of the family. We were both huge fans of the Osmonds, especially DONNY. Our bedrooms became shrines to him, and since purple was his favourite colour we wore it as often as possible. In my case the bedroom shrine caused a few problems as Jane preferred David Cassidy. I tried to convert her and explained that Donny was gorgeous and Cassidy was not only ugly but also couldn't sing. For some reason that made her very angry and resulted in a long-running fight between us. We eventually reached a truce and split the room right down the middle with her horrible posters on one side and mine at the other.

I had very wide-ranging taste in music then, and I enjoyed everything from Donny to Alice Cooper and David Bowie. I remember one strange obsession with a song called 'The Wheel of Fortune' by Kay Starr. It was an old 78 and I loved it. I can't remember why, but I played it over and over again and got on everyone's nerves until it disappeared. I suspected everyone but no one owned up to throwing it out.

One of the biggest thrills of my life was going to the

Apollo to see the Osmonds in concert. It was amazing, the atmosphere was electric and I screamed and cried through the whole thing. I've been to other concerts but nothing came close to the excitement of that night. Two years ago my wee daughter went to see East 17 for the first time, and although she is only eight, the way her face was all lit up when she came home took me right back to the Apollo. That night when she was asleep along with her brother and dad, I looked out the only old Donny tape I've still got and played it again. It sounded old fashioned and soppy but I enjoyed the memories.

Joyce and I spent hours listening to music and talking, mostly about boys, school and Donny. We would sit in either my room or hers and when it was time to go home we'd walk each other to the halfway point, the pillar box in Lochdochart Road just at Dalilea Drive. One night I walked Joyce to the box and as usual we stood for ages talking, and just as she turned to go home we both noticed a five pound note on the road. We used it to go to Shuffles disco in the town that weekend and never told anyone in case we had to hand it in to the police station.

Shuffles was in Sauchiehall Street, but it wasn't like other discos because it had no bar, so we could go at sixteen and our mums were quite happy. Mind you, they didn't know we sometimes sneaked cider into the toilets. We usually only had one small bottle between us, but the week we found the fiver we had one each and felt great until we went outside and we were both sick. We stuck to Coke for ages after that.

At this time dad worked on the lorries that delivered fish to the market. The lorry arrived from Aberdeen at about three in the morning and the driver and his mate picked my dad up at our house, so he always had their breakfast ready, which was very handy for us all after an exhausting night at Shuffles on a Friday. We ate with them and told them all about our night (except the cider). Then when they left for the market we went to bed.

I loved dad working with the fish as I've always shared his love for all kinds of seafood. We never tired of it. When he'd been working there for a while he worked out a way to get the best fish at the cheapest prices. He brought it home and weighed it into pounds and I wrapped it. We then sold it in Commonhead and in the Wee Brig Bar, a great pub that used to be before the train station where the motorway bridge is now. The man that owned it was Jimmy Young, a good friend of dad's who got his fish free. When the pub was demolished to make way for the motorway they put up a plaque for Jimmy and he bought a pub in Paisley. Dad really enjoyed the last night in the Brig and he took lots of photos which he often looked through, but he was sad to see the place go and had to go to Baillieston for a drink after that as the only other pub near us was the Casbah and he didn't like it.

As I said, dad was an Orangeman, and every year we'd march behind the bands at walks and church parades. The highlight of the year was the Bog Walk. When I was about fifteen, we walked to Glasgow Green. By this time Joyce had joined the Lodge too, and when we reached the park we collapsed on the grass intending to stay there until it was time to march back to Dennistoun. I fell asleep, and when I woke up Joyce was sitting up and talking to a guy

I'd never seen before. I thought he was chatting her up but it turned out he was her older brother Tony. They hadn't seen each other for five years and it was nice to see them together again. Tony was in a band, he played the accordion, and even better their dad was in the band too. Joyce was really looking forward to seeing her dad again, but she had to wait as he'd left the park already. We arranged to meet Tony at the Ibrox church parade the following week and he promised not to tell his dad as Joyce wanted to surprise him. The look on his face was a picture and they all cried. I did too, it was very moving. After a while Tony and I went for a walk to let Joyce and her dad talk. We got on quite well and enjoyed each other's company. He became my first really serious boyfriend but not for quite a while later.

The situation in Joyce's family was very complicated and private, so for various reasons we never mentioned meeting Tony or her dad to her mum. My parents knew, and sometimes Tony visited Joyce at my house. We quite often went to see him in Springburn, and soon everyone presumed we were an item but he was so shy it was actually over a year after we met before he kissed me. I wasn't too worried about this though, as Joyce and I were still enjoying ourselves every weekend and I didn't want to be tied down to anyone anyway.

My dad never liked Tony. He called him a waster and a big skinny chancer (among other things). I suppose dad was right, but I was young and I thought he was wonderful. It wasn't his fault he was always skint and was for ever in and out of dead-end jobs.

I left school as soon as I could and was lucky enough

to get a job straight away in the Clydesdale Bank. I
worked in the stationery department, where we printed
everything you use in the bank including cheque books
and travellers cheques. It was a great job and I stayed there
for nearly ten years.

Tony never stuck a job for very long, so I was amazed
when he came in one day and announced that he'd
joined the army. I was devastated, but he was determined
to go. He was six feet tall so he joined the Scots Guards
and had left for Surrey within a week. I cried buckets and
saw him off at Central Station with Joyce and her mum,
who by this time knew about us. The three of us went
home very sad and talked about how much we would
miss him, but it was short-lived and he was back home in
three days. I was delighted as I thought he'd changed his
mind, but he hadn't and when he left next time he was
away for three months' basic training. We soon settled into
the routine of seeing each other for a few days or weeks
at a time and it was all right really as I worked with a
great crowd and we sent each other lots of letters.

I now think that going out with Tony was like a
comfortable habit, we got engaged but didn't really make
any plans, we just seemed to plod on. I think I was in love
with the idea of being in love but was too young to really
know what I wanted. By then I had left the Lodge and
Tony had served in Ireland. We saw what people do in the
name of religion and didn't like it. I was used to getting
loads of letters, so I knew something was wrong when he
stopped writing. I fretted for weeks before he finally
plucked up the courage to write and tell me the truth. He
had been seeing someone else for months, she was a lot

older than him, was divorced and had four kids. I completely fell apart, and one person was there to see me through it, my dad. He was great and never once said 'I told you so'.

During that time my dad and I went out quite a lot to The Union Jack social club in Baillieston. We knew almost everyone who went and had some really good nights. One night dad went to the 'Jack' on his own, and when he got home (very late) he was in a pretty terrible state, he had two black eyes and his face was cut and swollen. He was also pretty drunk and wouldn't tell us what had happened only saying that he'd fell. He kept the story up until a week or two later when I discovered the truth. We went to the club on the Sunday afternoon and had just sat down when in walked three of the regulars, they spotted us and all called out 'HIGH HO SILVER AWAY'. The truth was out. Dad had been walking home on his own and as usual he'd stopped to pet the big horse in the field (where Springfield Farm is now). He then had a brilliant idea, it would be much better to ride home than walk. The horse was willing and everything went well until they reached the hedge at the end of the field. The horse stopped, dad went over the hedge and the crowd of so-called mates at the back had seen the lot. They checked he was all right and made sure he got home, but he was too drunk to remember talking to them and thought no one knew. We never let him forget it.

About three weeks later Tony wrote again saying how sorry he was and could he come home? I ignored the letter and all the others that arrived daily until I got one from his girlfriend accusing me of begging Tony to leave her and trying to split them up. I was so glad I had kept his letters and tied them up with a nice ribbon and posted them to her house with a note telling her to make up her own mind. I never heard from any of them again, although Joyce told me they eventually got married and went on to have three more kids. What a lucky escape that turned out to be.

After that experience, I didn't want serious boyfriends and had a good time going out with workmates, but I've stayed friendly with Joyce and the rest of her family over the years, especially her mum. Joyce has two kids and lives in Ireland, but her mum still lives here.

One of my friends in the bank had recently booked a holiday in Spain with her boyfriend, but they had fallen out and she asked if I would like to go. I counted the cost and had four months to save some spending money, so I said yes. We had an exciting time shopping for new clothes and doing overtime so that we would have enough money. She very quickly got over her boyfriend and was soon seeing someone else. She met Davie at a party and I met Alan the same night. Alan was really nice, but I went out with a few guys and wasn't serious about any of them. He was the hearts and flowers type and kept talking about 'our future'. This really put me off him, so when my pal said Davie's brother was home after a year in France and she wanted someone to make up a foursome I jumped at the chance.

Davie wasn't too pleased to see me when we walked into Sloans restaurant that night as he was Alan's friend and knew how he felt about me, but his brother Colin and I got on really well. The following week Alan had a party and I left with Colin. We started seeing a lot of each other, but there was no pressure, we were both quite happy as things were. I was looking forward to Spain, and Colin wanted to go back to France as he was only home for a while to get some money together. He bought a motorbike and we went out on it all the time. Alan was very upset and made me promise to phone him when I got back from Spain in case I changed my mind. Colin rode out to the airport to see us off, and as I got on the plane I decided not to bother phoning any of them when I came home. I surprised myself by missing Colin an awful lot. It was a brilliant holiday, but I was pleased to get home and delighted when Colin phoned to ask me out that night.

I saw Alan the following week and told him we were finished and explained that I only went about with Colin because he, like me, wasn't interested in getting engaged or married. Colin and I will celebrate our fifteenth wedding anniversary this year!

The 13th of May 1980 started like any other day, but before it was over I had gone through one of the worst days of my life. Colin had stayed over at our house and we left for work together. By tea-time I got a phone call from his aunt Mary. She said Colin had been involved in an accident at work (he was a fork-lift driver in a foundry in Maryhill). She said it was bad and that he was in the Western Infirmary. I asked if I could phone back and speak to his mum as the phone I was on was next to the machines and I couldn't hear very well. That wasn't really true but I needed time to take it all in. I felt panicky and didn't know what to do.

Colin's mum was in tears when I spoke to her. She had been told Colin had broken his leg, arm, shoulder, ribs and collarbone. He also had a punctured lung and was losing a lot of blood. I got to the hospital just as they were taking his parents in to see him but I had to wait in a side room with Colin's sister and her husband. A doctor came and told us Colin had been driving the fork-lift when a false floor gave way. It fell twenty-five feet and Colin had been trapped underneath. The doctor confirmed all of the injuries and also said they were worried about his leg as the bone had come through his skin and was broken in three places but they couldn't operate on it yet as there was a valve in his heart that wouldn't close. An ambulance was on standby to take him to the Royal for surgery.

Thankfully it wasn't needed and we were eventually allowed in to see him. He was in intensive care and was wired up to machines. There seemed to be tubes and wires everywhere. I was terrified. I honestly thought he would die. That night seemed to last for ever, and I think that was when I admitted to myself how much I loved him. Colin was told he'd be in hospital for months, but he amazed everyone, including the doctors. He was in a general ward within two weeks and back home after another two. He had a special fibre plaster on his left leg, which is badly scarred, and he also has scars under his left arm, his forehead and his side. He knows how lucky he was to survive the accident but still suffers a lot of pain and naturally gets frustrated at not being able to do things as he used to.

He was back at work just before Christmas that year, but before that he went through months of physiotherapy. I've always admired his courage but sometimes get annoyed because he refuses to take things easy when he's in pain and walks everywhere when it seems easier to take a bus. I'm happier now because he doesn't work any more. He went on Invalidity in 1994. Our doctor had been telling him to leave work long before that, but he was determined not to stop.

It would have been easy for Colin to just sit back and do nothing, but that's not in his nature. He spends lots of time with the kids and does all the things with them that my dad did with me. Last year he decided to go to college to do a course in computing, both to learn for himself and also because our son gets computing at school and Colin wants to be able to understand what his homework meant.

We got married on 19 February 1982 at Martha Street Registry Office. Our reception was in Partick Burgh Halls, and it was the best party ever. Colin and I stayed on to the very end, everyone kept asking when we were leaving but we were enjoying it too much. We didn't have a honeymoon as we decided to use our money to put a bigger deposit on our flat. The flat was in Anniesland and we loved it. It had very high ceilings and huge bay windows.

Most of our neighbours were working couples and we got on well, but after I had our son we began to feel quite lonely and cut off from our families. Anniesland didn't feel like home any more. We thought about moving, but in the end fate decided for us. I had left work before Aaron was born, and when he was two months old Colin was made redundant. We couldn't afford the mortgage payments so decided to move back to Easterhouse.

We moved into Glassel Road, and although I felt at
home it took Colin some time to adjust. He was brought
up in Dalmuir and had heard all sorts of horror stories
about Drummy Land. Colin soon settled in and got to
know everyone. That was in 1984 and four years later Jill
was born. Colin was now working in a distillery and I was
at home with the kids. I loved them to bits but I was
bored stiff. I had been on the school council as a parent
rep for Aaron's nursery, but now he was at school and I
had a new baby in the house. Colin persuaded me to join
the parent helpers group in Bishoploch School and that's
how I started my new life as a volunteer. The parent
helpers was made up of a core of about six regulars and
they made me feel really welcome. We helped out
wherever we were needed, in the library, playroom and
book club. We also worked with the kids on art projects
and went along to help on school trips.

Through the parent helper group I also got involved in
the Lochwood Church Playgroup which was both
enjoyable and practical as Jill was still a toddler. My next
adventure into the unknown was the newly formed
school board at Bishoploch. For this I had to write
something about myself to be sent to all the parents so
that they could decide whether or not to vote for me at
the election. There were six candidates and only four
could succeed. I was terrified. I was fortunate enough to
win that election and apart from allowing me almost four
years of insight into how much hard work goes on in our
schools and a lot of fun, it also gave me a great deal of
confidence in myself. I realized that I was capable of
making decisions, working with others and speaking to

all sorts of groups and individuals without feeling intimidated. I also learned that to get what you want you don't have to be confrontational, just sure of your facts and determined.

Everyone I worked with at that time played a part in bringing out that confidence, but none more so than the head teacher at Bishoploch. By always listening to my suggestions and answering my questions she made me feel useful and part of the team. She respected my opinion and I shall always be grateful to her. One of the most nerve-racking things I had to do on the school board was to address the parents at a public meeting. I was nervous but I managed it OK. The next job was the worst I ever had, it was to be part of the interview panel to select a new assistant head. That experience was to prove invaluable later, but at the time I felt completely out of my depth and a bit of a fake, after all how could I interview teachers? I took comfort from the fact that the candidates were more nervous than I was and we eventually decided on one who is still doing a great job, so we must have made the right decision.

Being so closely involved with the school has given me an insight not many parents are allowed in a huge part of their kids' lives, and because of that I am confident they are getting the best care and attention possible, which is a nice thought. I believe I would still be as involved today if events hadn't forced a change.

In 1990, the local tenants association called a public meeting. The flyers were full of stuff like 'Do you want a new house?' and 'Are you happy with the service you get from the council?' Like everyone else I thought 'What service?' and went along to the meeting thinking I was in for a new house. We couldn't be more wrong. We sat there and listened to the depressing news that not only did the council know how bad our houses were but they also admitted they had no plans or money to make them any better. Both future plans and future funding for Lochend were NIL.

The next speaker was from Scottish Homes whom I'd never heard of but she said there was something that may be possible – we could do something ourselves. We all sat and listened to her going on about housing associations and how we could buy the houses and manage them with a committee of tenants. Like many others I was sceptical and suspicious, but a few very brave people agreed to form a steering group to look at possibilities.

I went home feeling more depressed than ever about the deplorable state of our homes and had no faith in this latest scheme. We had heard many promises in the past that fell through and had no reason to believe this one was any different. I put it out of my mind and carried on as before. I was kept busy as Colin was working full time and I had the house, the kids, the school and the playgroup to worry about.

A couple of weeks later another meeting was called, this time by the steering group, so we went along to be nosy just like most folk. The spokeswoman from Scottish Homes spoke again, and this time I began to really listen. There was a lot of shouting going on and it was a bit rowdy, but the people who'd signed up at the first meeting were there and they wanted more of us to join them. By the end of the meeting I knew I had to join the steering group. I knew there was no point in waiting about for someone else to do the work, I had to find out more for myself.

We were and still are totally made up of volunteer tenants, and our collective knowledge of how to move forward was ZERO. We needed advice and training, and where to get it was our first assignment. The group looked at the options and decided to use Calvay Housing Co-op. They were based in Barlanark and had experienced similar problems to our own. If I had known then just how much I would become involved in this I honestly believe I would have run a mile, but it all happened so gradually I didn't notice it becoming so important in my life.

We started meeting every Tuesday night for training. One of the first things we learned was that as one door opens another one slams in your face! I soon found to my surprise that I was actually quite good at fighting our corner, especially when the opponent was an official. Which was just as well as we had reason to fight every other week. Gradually things started to make sense to us and thanks to the excellent help and support we received we realized we were actually capable of forming a housing co-operative. We commissioned consultants to do a feasibility study of our area which consisted of 531 tenement flats, most of which were three-apartments. Having convinced ourselves it would work we then had to convince everyone else. Many times we felt like giving up but, eventually, in April 1993 we were registered with Scottish Homes.

Four years down the line we still meet every Tuesday night and I still fight with officials, but it has been so

worthwhile. Between Re-hab and New Build we have so
far provided 150 homes in Lochend. There is still a long
way to go and with constant cuts to the housing budget
things don't get any easier but we WILL finish the job.

In March this year Colin and I finally moved into
OUR new house, and I can now say with certainty that
I know how my parents felt thirty-eight years ago when
they moved out here. We may not have been impressed
by the inside toilet, but we were absolutely delighted with
the double glazing, central heating, fitted kitchen, extra
bedroom, back and front doors, dining room and even a
fully floored loft.

I'd like to say things were perfect now for us, but life's
not that kind. Three years ago my dad died of cancer, he
was only sixty-four years old. Everyone loves their dad,
but mine was so special, he was such a large part of my
life and nothing will ever fill that void. Later the same
year Colin's mum also died. I can't say how we coped, we
just did. Nothing is the same now and we know it never
will be, but at least we came through it together. Two very
special people have gone from our lives, but I know they
would be happy for us and I think they would want us to
stay here in Easterhouse because as far as I'm concerned
THINGS CAN ONLY GET BETTER.

*Notes*
1. Broo: unemployment benefit
2. Single end: one-room tenement building
3. Greet: weep
4. Skelp: slap
5. Sannie: sandshoe

# Part 3

# Faith in the Poor

At a book launch in London, I met a senior member of one of Britain's leading publishers. She later told me that the idea of a book by poor people would not find a trade publisher and she advised me to publish it privately and try to recoup the costs by selling it in the community. Her attitude reflects the one I summarized in the first part of this book. Those who control the outlets of communication may express sympathy towards people with low incomes who dwell in the inner cities and estates, but they are not prepared to give them a voice. They imply that their efforts are only good enough for local consumption. The barrier they erect is based partly on their assumption that those in what Will Hutton calls the bottom 30 per cent lack the ability to write. The contributors to this volume challenge that assumption.

The evocative piece by Cynthia lovingly recalls the Easterhouse of its early years when children still played in the peat fields and burns; she remembers the happiness brought to children by pets and by traditional games in the open air and in the closes; she depicts the Orange lodges, the marches, the sectarian gatherings; she movingly describes her close relationship with her lorry-driving dad; she catches her teenage years and her boyfriends and how she marries Colin despite his horrific accident at work; finally she writes about her own gradual and increasing involvement in local projects. Cynthia captures so much of what is the essence of Glasgow: children playing in the streets, the sectarian divides, tough but good parents, the financial struggles of marriage when they could not afford the mortgage, serious accidents at work, a readiness to support local action. Cynthia can write and write well.

It might be countered that Cynthia is exceptional, that she is one of the Easterhouse successes who had a stable background, happy marriage and made it to a nice house with a housing co-operative. Many other Easterhouse residents are likewise stable and well married. But even if they are not, this does not mean they cannot write. The other contributors have experienced disruption and poverty. Carol reveals both the despair of a single mother whose child is taken from her and the courage of regaining her. Anita portrays the distress imposed by waves of tragedies along with her struggles to survive. Erica tells, in almost a matter-of-fact way, how she was abused as a child, how she drifted into prostitution, and how she came out of it into a life of poverty. Penny details horrific ups and downs, the ups of loving her children, the downs of being cruelly treated and harassed by her drug-abusing partner. Denise records a childhood of being in and out of care and an early adulthood of coping with three small children with little money and poor housing. Bill's words somehow get lighter when he mentions the clubs and holidays he enjoyed yet grow darker as he moves into unemployment and a police cell. The conclusion is clear. Easterhouse people can write. My experience is that many others in their positions can do likewise. People in poverty can write. Their exclusion from the press, from TV and radio, from books, is not because they cannot articulate. Rather it is because they are not allowed access. Their voices deserve to be heard for they have much to say. At least the publishers of this book have been justified in their faith in the poor.

## Perspectives from the poor

So people on low incomes can write. For the rest of the book, I wish to draw together their writings in order to see what they say about a range of subjects. In so doing, I will make links between what the contributors say and the views and studies of outside sources. I hope I am well placed to undertake this task by virtue of having a foot in both camps. Easterhouse has been my home for the last twelve years. I have known the writers as neighbours, as participants in the activities of the Salvation Army and FARE and, in most cases, as friends. Simultaneously, I have continued my contacts with universities and politics. In this section, I will bring the two worlds together to comment on the reality of poverty, to challenge the notion of an underclass, to consider how the contributors have managed to survive, and to assess the relevance of social work. Later I will focus on the role of the Christian church before concluding with some implications for the future.

## The reality of poverty

Not all residents of inner cities and council estates are poor. Cynthia was brought up in a family where her father was in employment, her husband too had a job until the results of an accident at work became too much for him. She certainly did not have an easy time and, at one point, had to move from a purchased flat back to Easterhouse to housing conditions which were not adequate. Cynthia and her husband are certainly not well-off compared with many citizens in Britain. None the less, they have had sufficient to ensure a stable life for their children.

However, many residents are on very low incomes. Recent research by the Rowntree Foundation points out that, excluding pensioners, around half the households in council estates do not have anyone in employment.[1] They are dependent upon state benefits. Carol comes into this category. As a single mother, she struggled financially. After marriage, her husband was often unemployed, but Carol qualified for disability living allowance and this, allied with her budgetary skills, enabled her to adequately furnish the council flat and feed and clothe their children. None the less, the flat contains much dampness.

The contributors were not given a specific brief about what to write. They were asked to put down what they found interesting and considered important to them. Cynthia and Carol gave few details about their financial position. The other five writers did devote attention to their financial struggles and recorded their weekly incomes from income support. Erica and her family received £118.79; Denise and her family £76.20; Penny and her children £81.60; Anita and her children £79.50. In addition they would have qualified for housing benefit. Bill received £28.50. In Britain, poverty has been taken as the condition of those living on or below the basic income support levels. More recently, the measure used in much of Western Europe has gained acceptance, namely that of those dependent upon incomes below half of the average income of the country concerned. The five who gave their details were poor by both these measures. Indeed, the four with children were not receiving their full entitlements. Taking into account income support, the family premium and single-parent premium, I calculated that the families were receiving £7–£40 less than their dues. The main explanation was that they had taken out social fund loans which were repaid by automatic deductions from their weekly incomes.

The incomes of the four families who gave financial details were thus below basic rates. They were in poverty. Their plight cannot be attributed to extravagance. Apart from Erica's cigs (of which more will be said later), they spent their money on the barest essentials. Penny explained that her money went on 'food, the council tax, powercards, stamps for the TV, a card for the light meter'. Erica's detailed accounts reveal similar items plus clothing and bus fares. None possessed freezers or cars, so it was impossible to travel to big supermarkets to bulk-buy cheap goods for storage. Instead, they relied upon local shops and mobile shops where food prices tended to be high. The families were poor despite being financially careful.

The writers are not self-pitying or bitter. In straightforward terms, they tell about the depth and extent of their poverty in words which come across more strongly than some polished academic reports composed by well-heeled outsiders. They reveal three major components of poverty: hardship, powerlessness and monotony.

The families who wrote about their finances suffered definite *hardship*. Denise and her partner really did have bare boards at the start, and continued to survive on secondhand clothes and furniture. Penny went to charity shops for her children's clothes, adding 'I cannot afford to go into a proper shop like Poundstretchers or British Home Stores.' Even secondhand clothes have to be washed, but Penny did not possess a washing machine. At times, Erica's budget did not run to a gas token, so the family endured a cold home and a lack of hot water for a bath. They did not starve, but the diet was restricted to hamburgers, corned beef, tinned meat, potatoes, eggs, beans, margarine, bread, milk, sugar and tea. Fresh fruit, vegetables and meat did not appear. And by the end of the week, a meal might consist of a single slice of bread.

It was the hardships endured by the children which most hurt the parents. Anita complained, 'My children hardly go out of Easterhouse. I cannot afford to give them the things they need like nice clothes and nice bedrooms. I would like them to have all these things and to take them on holidays, but it is impossible on social security.' Erica's children had not been on a holiday for seven years. One of her daughters was upset when there was no money to go to a disco. The children of these families did not go to the recreational facilities taken for granted by so many children. Perhaps most painfully Erica could not afford the registration fee which would have been the starting-point to search for her adopted son. The inability of the parents to spend on their children clearly meant hardship for them. It also meant that the children were forced into lifestyles drastically different from those whose parents are comfortably off. Research published by the Rowntree Foundation shows that, on average, parents spend about £2,700 on their children each year. If Erica's family (the one with highest income amongst the writers) divided their income equally among all its members, then the children could only receive £1,031 a year. In Denise's family it would be £800. The study also showed that parents spent significant amounts on educational aides such as books, school trips and extra lessons. For those at secondary school it was, on average, £5.92 a week.[2] The contributors to this book could not afford a pound a week. The hardships their children suffered in comparison with the advantages of others are yet another example of the inequalities in Britain.

Poverty is not just material hardship. It is also *powerlessness*, the sense of lacking the means to counter that hardship. Erica and her husband wanted to buy decent Christmas presents for their children. Like many low-incomed parents, they received pressure from their children to buy the goodies advertised on TV, the kind of presents which so many other children do get. Unfortunately, Erica and her husband lacked sufficient income to buy such presents and could not obtain low–interest loans through banks or legal money-lenders. Economically, they were powerless. They reacted by borrowing £220 from a loan shark. The children got some presents, but the shark's high interest rates, enforced by the threat of violence, meant they had to repay £450 and were so plunged even further into the abyss of poverty. Erica explained, 'It was robbery but I had no other option.'

Anita did not turn to the sharks and settled for less. At Christmas, she usually obtained some presents from the Salvation Army. She has also been helped by a journalist who interviewed her years ago. Unlike some journalists, this one was not content to extract information and disappear. She built a relationship with the family, wrote letters, and provided Christmas presents. But, outside of Christmas, Anita constantly borrows. She wrote, 'I can't get by from week to week without borrowing. I don't like asking people. I always get one of the kids to ask for me... I did once ask the [Social Work] Department for help. It was very hard. I had to swallow my pride. I felt as though I was begging. I felt very degraded and low when they refused me. Nobody knows how bad I was feeling after being turned down.' Poverty forced Anita into actions which she hated to do. Powerlessness.

Not least, the writers showed that they had little control over their accommodation. After her turbulent early life, Erica married and settled in Easterhouse, but felt she had to leave because of the racial insults suffered by two of her children. The family made for Wakefield in England, but its Housing Department refused to help on the grounds that they did not have sufficient reason for leaving their Easterhouse flat. Erica, her husband and four children were on the streets until her brother took them into his one-bedroomed flat. The gross overcrowding caused by this action seemed to force the officials' hand and a home was found for them. Unfortunately, the racism was just as strong and Erica moved the family to Bradford where she understood her children would be accepted. Here a private landlord conned them into taking a single room. Erica felt defeated and helpless. She overdosed and her children went into public care. Finally the family was rehoused and reunited, but only after experiences which must have taken a toll on their physical and emotional health.

Anita was living in a flat sodden with damp and where I have seen, in winter, bedrooms decorated with both fungi and ice. But her desperation to move from the district sprang more from a sense of oppression and fear. Her tears were almost evident as she wrote, 'I dread to think what the future holds for my kids if I don't get away from Easterhouse soon while they are still young, I know in my heart they will either turn to drugs or end up in prison.' Anita asked the Housing Department for a transfer but was offered similar properties in similar districts. She explored private renting but found it beyond her means. She felt trapped. Powerless. Finally the council did agree to move the family near to her ailing father. They went to a larger and drier flat but in a location where drugs, crime and unemployment were still rife. Anita was not primarily worried about the size of the flat. She longed to bring up her children in a street where the forces would not handicap her children. It proved impossible. Powerless.

Penny is still in her thirties. In her lifetime she has gone through a bewildering number of moves. Her motherhood started in a homeless unit before the council moved her to a flat in Easterhouse. The mild Penny was soon being harassed by neighbours and took refuge with a girlfriend before being offered a safer tenancy. Unfortunately she had to leave as it was being demolished. Her next home was with her partner, but there followed a tale of horror as his debts led to threats and attacks which compelled them to flee. Her reward for sticking with her partner was that he became so violent that she had to flee from him. For years, Penny never seemed able to secure a place where she could be safe and settled.

Denise is even younger than Penny. In her own childhood, she must have felt like a human ping-pong ball as she went between various relatives and institutions. Once she became pregnant, the authorities gave her a shabby flat in Easterhouse. After eight months she was moved into another flat nearby. This building was eventually demolished so resulting in another move to a flat where she feels a virtual prisoner. She is powerless to obtain more money, powerless to change her circumstances, powerless to look after her children in the way she wants.

Denise's life is dull and repetitive, for poverty can mean *monotony*. She wrote, 'I am stuck in most of the time.' She takes the children to school, shops when the van comes round, cooks a meal and watches TV. A highlight is a visit to bingo. None of the contributors mentioned going to the cinema or out for a meal. Erica stated, 'I didn't want to get up today because I felt so fed up with my life. It's the same thing day-in, day-out. I don't get to go out with Ivor or on my own because we can't afford it. I don't know the last time we went out together.' No doubt, some will condemn Erica for smoking. But for her it was a relief from boredom, from the monotony of a life that was insular, restricted and repetitive. She said, 'I hate it that people say that because you are on social security you shouldn't smoke. But it's like Valium, it calms me.' Noticeably both Erica and Anita – who lived a similar monotonous existence – had seriously considered taking their own lives

Bill, unlike the others, is not a parent, but, being unemployed, he spends much time in the house and is bored. He recorded, 'I get up at about eleven o'clock and go downstairs and see my mum, have a cup of tea and make some breakfast. Then I go and see if any of my pals are out on the street. If not I just sit and watch the telly. In the evening I might go and play football. I used to go to the raves at the Tenants' Hall but there was a lot of fighting and I stopped going. I get depressed sometimes.' Like the others, Bill was in a disadvantaged area which lacked recreational facilities. He lacked the money to travel to and partake in commercial entertainment. He could not afford home amusements like a computer. One day became very like another. Poverty meant monotony.

The written accounts by these contributors can hardly

be described as academic research. But they do consist of a living comment on the work of outside commentators in three directions.

First, they are a rebuke to those who preach that the problem of poverty is exaggerated. Adrian Rogers, Director of the Conservative Family Institute, claimed that income support rates are 'pretty lavish'.[3] Richard Pryke, writing for the Institute of Economic Affairs, asserted that the proportion of the population in poverty 'is negligible' and 'since mass poverty does not exist, there is no call for the feelings of guilt which are generated by its supposed existence'. He even implies that people on very low incomes are not generally made unhappy by this.[4] The details given by Erica, Anita, Denise and Penny reveal that life on income support meant a hand-to-mouth existence, reliance on secondhand furniture and clothes, continual debt, choices between paying bills or buying food, and lacking the money to keep warm. The tensions and anxieties associated with their hardship and monotony led to depression, unhappiness, illness and distress. Their poverty is real and cannot be wished away by the words of affluent politicians and academics. Moreover, these contributors are not alone. Anyone who lives in inner-city areas or peripheral estates knows that their lot is that of thousands. Indeed, around 9 million people are dependent upon income support.

Second, the vivid words of the contributors confirm surveys which identify the undermining effect of the social fund. Prior to 1988, people dependent upon social security were entitled to what were called 'single-payment grants' to replace worn-out essential items like cookers, fires and fridges. In order to cut the amount spent on these grants, the government, as part of the Social Security Act (1986), replaced most of the grants with social fund loans by which claimants could request a loan which was discretionary. If granted, it was repaid by compulsory deductions from their weekly income support. Research by Fran Bennett and her colleagues suggested that many applicants did not obtain the loans and so were deprived of domestic goods which are now considered a part of decent living while others obtained loans but faced drastic cuts in their incomes.[5] The contributors to this book well illustrate what happens. Denise obtained a social fund loan and had £10 a week taken from her measly income. Erica knew she would not get a social fund loan and so turned to a private loan shark. Penny had an official loan for bedding but was refused a further one for a washing machine. Anita took out social fund loans but then found that the weekly deductions made it difficult to support a family of four on £79.90. She argued, 'In my opinion a grant should be given for important things. I can hardly feed my kids let alone clothe them, yet I know there is no point in applying for another loan for clothes.'

Third, the experiences of the contributors include examples of the psycho-social effects of inequality as put forward by Richard Wilkinson. Professor Wilkinson acknowledges that poverty entails material hardship. He adds that in Britain, especially since 1979, the poor have got poorer within an affluent society. In other words, inequality has increased. He then argues that for those at the bottom, this inequality generates feelings of failure, inferiority and powerlessness. They see themselves as losers in a society where others are winning, with success being judged in terms of money. Individuals deal with these intense feelings by what he calls psycho-social mechanisms which lead to behaviour characterized by apathy, withdrawal, depression and aggression. Such behaviour then serves to make even worse the conditions and circumstances of those concerned.[6]

Certainly, Erica, Denise Anita, Penny and, at times, Carol felt excluded from mainstream society. They did react with apathy, depression and withdrawal which made it even harder for them to cope. Bill, it appears, reacted to his long-term unemployment and monotony with aggression. Sad to report, he is now in prison following a serious act of violence. Wilkinson's deduction is that if major social problems are to be tackled then it is not enough just to alleviate poverty. In addition, greater equality is required so that a more united and coherent society is promoted with no citizens feeling they do not belong. My own observations do back Wilkinson's theory. Many poverty-stricken people are made to feel worthless and powerless and have to find ways of dealing with their feelings. However, this is not to say that they are always dominated by negative reactions, by their depressions and withdrawals. At times they react with a determination to fight back.

## Strong people

The contributors do record many lows in their lives. They did experience despair, anger, sadness, breakdowns, even thoughts of suicide. Yet one of the perceptions that emerges from their words is that within all these traumas and apparent weaknesses, they are also strong people.

Consider Cynthia. She was born in a tenement flat 'with outside, shared toilets, open back courts and lots of large families crammed into small rooms'. The family moved to better housing in Easterhouse, but initially her parents had to travel miles to purchase cheap food for their five children. Most clothes were secondhand, and holidays consisted of a day out at Helensburgh. After marriage, Cynthia and her husband could not afford their mortgage and moved back to council accommodation in Easterhouse. Later her husband had to give up work. Despite these setbacks, Cynthia emerges as a stable woman who faced difficulties with equanimity. A strong person.

Consider Erica. Her mum died when she was young, so leaving her to sexual abuse by her stepfather. She was taken into the care of the local authority and drifted into prostitution. Aged fifteen she bore a child. At seventeen she was pregnant again. She went to prison and, on coming out, got pregnant once more. Life improved when she married, but her husband did have drink problems. They were homeless and in constant poverty. Erica's own children went into care for a while. Her eldest daughter was raped. At times Erica was suicidal. Yet Erica survived. She and her husband united the family. She is not bitter and she still laughs. She has views, can discuss, can write. There are probably members of the House of Commons with public school and Oxbridge advantages who would have been broken if subjected to what Erica has gone through. A strong person.

Consider Anita. As a child, she had periods in a children's home. As a wife and mother she knew little but social deprivations. Her husband committed suicide just before she gave birth to her seventh child. Her two oldest girls were removed into care. Her eldest son lurched into heroin addiction. Anita often withdrew into isolation and depression. Her other sons displayed behavioural problems. To cap it all her closest brother died of cancer. Yet Anita has endured and has constantly striven for her children. A strong person.

Much the same could be said of Carol, Denise and Penny. They faced personal traumas, rejections, deprivations enough to overwhelm anyone. Yet they did not run away, did not abandon their children. Poor people but strong people.

At the start of this book, attention was drawn to Charles Murray's conception of the underclass. He blames much poverty, immorality and crime on a growing number of feckless young men and women: the men choose not to work and opt to take drugs, which pushes them into crime: the young women choose to have babies but not to live with male partners, they are irresponsible towards their children who therefore grow up wild, delinquent and work-shy and so perpetuate the next round of poverty. Murray takes Easterhouse as a home of the underclass.[7] His understanding of the place and its people appear to be based on one short visit. And this is the weakness of Murray's approach. He presents a snapshot of certain poor people and then concludes that the characteristics displayed by them at that moment are their prevailing features. By contrast, the contributors to this book present themselves over many years and so bring very different perceptions about the people of Easterhouse and about poverty.

A Charles Murray snapshot could present Carol as a single mum who gives up the care of her child, Anita as the apathetic mum who breeds a heroin addict, Erica as a prostitute who bore children by different fathers, Penny as a non-worker who stays in the homeless hostel, Denise as the young mum who lounges about indoors, Bill as the workless young thug. Murray could portray them as evidence of the underclass, weak characters whose lack of morals and motivation lead to their poverty and malfunctioning and who are a threat to the nation. But, seen from the perspectives they present over a long timescale, then they come over as strong people, who overcome enormous setbacks, who care desperately for their children and who succeed in bringing them up. Even Bill emerges as a teenager who wants work, who refuses drugs and who is reluctantly pulled into crime by boredom and circumstances. The deduction is that the contributors are not an underclass whose difficulties stem from their wickedness, neglect of children and a rejection of work. Rather they have to be regarded as people born into many disadvantages and whose efforts to survive are handicapped by conditions of deprivation and poverty. Far from creating poverty, they were flung into it. Given the incomes and surroundings of more affluent citizens, the contributors could have avoided much of the distress and want which became the lot of their children.

## The secrets of survival

The writers were strong people. Even so, at times they faced personal storms which would have destroyed the strongest. How did they survive? In the end, the answer must be that each possessed a *resolve to endure*. For some, this was expressed in a certain turning point, a moment when they determined to fight. Erica recorded that with her child taken from her and struggling with a drinking problem, 'I looked at my mirror and I didn't like what I saw. I decided to sort out my life before I lost another child.' Penny was walking the streets and considering whether to take her own life when she decided that she just had to build a life for her baby. Carol's daughter was in care and she was attending her eighth birthday party when the social worker said to her, 'Enjoy it because it's your last.' This painful remark moved Carol to fight to get her back.

These personal decisions, however, were not made in a vacuum. From the writings, it becomes possible to see that the decisions and what followed were strengthened by a number of *human support systems*. Erica had no living parents, but she entered into a true love relationship with a man and both he and his parents proved crucial in giving her meaning and encouragement. Carol had differences with her father but, as a single mother, she could often call upon him at times of crisis until she too met and married a man who was to be a tower of emotional strength. Penny also experienced some rejection from her parents when she informed them of her pregnancy, but later found some acceptance from them. Cynthia had the closest relationships to parents and husband, which partly explains why her life was the most stable. Denise and Anita probably had the least consistent support from close relatives. Denise's father was dead, but she did maintain some contact with and received some shelter with her mother and sister. Anita's mother was dead and her dad in poor health. However, Anita's grown-up daughters maintained contact with her. As children, most of the contributors had gone through difficult relationships with their own parents, and four of the seven spent some time in children's homes. None the less, links with them were maintained and proved vital. Today much concern is expressed about the family, and books are written about whether or not it has a future.[8] The lesson from these writers, who often faced turbulent family lives, is that the family is still the most enduring form of help, the unit to which members feel they can turn for help. It follows that, in terms of social policy, the first ploy should be to enable families to support their own members.

It was not just relatives that enabled the contributors to survive. Indeed, apart from Cynthia, all relied heavily upon supports from outside the family. The church was very important to some as will be discussed at a later point. Penny, Denise, Cynthia, Anita, Carol and Bill lived – at least for a period, for all moved homes – in an area where *local neighbourhood groups* were active. Neighbourhood groups encompass residents acting together in projects for the well-being of their community. The part of Easterhouse where the contributors dwelt included a credit union, a food co-operative, a housing co-operative, and a project, which has already been mentioned, called FARE. FARE (Family Action in Rogerfield and Easterhouse) was the one with which I am associated and runs youth clubs, holidays and support for vulnerable families.[9] These projects were important to the contributors for the following reasons.

First, they provided facilities for their children. Anita stated how important it was that Bill could play football and go to camps. He was able to develop his skills at football, table tennis and swimming, and Bill himself recorded how he was boosted when he won trophies at the clubs. At the camps he made relationships with leaders whom he could admire. Penny's son also benefited from attending the youth clubs in an area where there was no statutory or commercial provision for youth. Both families subsequently moved from the area and, it appears, the youngsters never found similar clubs where they could both spend their leisure time and know adults with whom to share problems.

Second, their staff were available. Statutory social workers tend to live outside of deprived zones and to commute in. They are around in office hours. The staff of neighbourhood projects often reside in the areas. Being neighbours, they get to know other residents closely. Further, they are available in the evenings, at weekends, on bank holidays. Carol, Denise, Penny and Anita all received some practical or skilled help from project workers, varying from conveying secondhand goods to negotiating with the Housing Department to being accompanied to a children's hearing. They also took advantage of their presence just to talk, to express anger, to share anxieties.

Third, they encouraged involvement. Statutory services can sometimes treat users just as recipients, those who receive but do not give. Neighbourhood groups put an emphasis on local involvement, and this particularly benefited Cynthia and Carol. Cynthia, somewhat to her own surprise, became a participant in a church playgroup and was then elected to the school board, where she found she could contribute to important decision-making and could speak in public. She was thus ready when a housing co-operative was formed and she became a key member who negotiated with officials, made plans and spoke with housing consultants. She not only moved into a new home with her family, she saw 150 good quality homes completed. As she said, earlier in her life she would never have dreamt of being in a house with double glazing, central heating and a fitted kitchen. Even less would she have dreamt that she would have been a human part of the process which was transforming her district. Involvement enabled Cynthia to see that she could achieve something worthwhile not just for herself but also for others.

Involvement was even more significant for Carol. As a young single mother, she felt rejected and demeaned. She had a poor image of herself, of her worth and of her abilities. Then, while her daughter was still in public care, she became a volunteer helper with the local food co-operative, where she participated in collecting the food, selling it, and looking after the accounts. She wrote, 'Later I was elected chairperson. It gave me a purpose... They respected me and it gave me more confidence.' After her daughter was returned and she was married and had more children, Carol became a leading and well-known member of the Easterhouse Breast Feeding Initiative, which was so successful that it won public awards. She wrote further, 'Over the years it has helped me to help others. I like helping people... I am a different person now from ten years ago.' Having known Carol over that ten years, I can testify to the difference. Initially her sense of inferiority was expressed both in a denial of her own goodness which prompted withdrawal and also in a volatile aggressiveness. Today these tendencies can still be seen, like scars of old wounds, yet generally she is a stable and confident parent, wife and member of the community. Some of this improvement appears to spring from the self-confidence she gained from being involved in local groups.

Carol's story confirms that of other studies which show that residents, often from very deprived backgrounds, achieve personal development when they know they are contributing to the common good. It also serves to counter one of the themes of Robert Whelan of the Institute of Economic Affairs, who claims that modern voluntary agencies do nothing to change needy people but merely collude with their problems.[10] With regard to the people in this book, voluntary neighbourhood groups combined with relatives in order to support the individual's own personal strengths. The outcome was that they managed to survive what were often horrific emotional traumas and socially difficult circumstances and often emerged, against all the odds, as whole families.

## Social work

Social workers also played a part in the survival. Families in the inner cities and peripheral estates often have contact with local authority social workers from the Social Work Departments (in Scotland) or the Social Services Departments (in England and Wales). Apart from Cynthia, all the contributors experienced their intervention. A great deal of research has been undertaken into social work. Indeed, Stirling University has a much respected Social Work Research Centre, which is devoted to such study. Here some recipients of social work are able to render their perspectives.

Erica, after spending a part of her childhood in institutions, had her first baby removed and placed for adoption by officials. She has never really come to terms with this decision, still misses her son, still longs to see him. She was fifteen when this occurred and, two years later, social workers placed her second child in a foster home. She regained that child, had another and then married the man by whom she had two more children. They struggled to hold their family together and, when living in one room in England, had varying experiences of social workers. One, in Erica's opinion, did nothing to help. The other related well with Erica. After serious discussion, they agreed together that three of the four children should be received into care but only on a temporary basis. The social worker then not only assisted Erica and her husband to obtain council accommodation but also helped to furnish it. Within a week the children came home as the social worker had promised. They probably came too soon and the social worker arranged further temporary care during which Erica visited her children regularly until they could return for good.

Anita's views were also mixed. Following her husband's tragic death, her two eldest girls went into care where a social worker supported them to achieve 'independent living'. Anita acknowledged 'everything has worked out great for my two girls'. On the other hand, Anita never co-operated well with the social workers who often came to visit her family. She felt she was not understood by them and declared, 'Nobody knows how I feel except myself because I can't talk to anybody about it.' She considered that the social workers investigated her but did not offer any practical aid. She stated, 'I have been at a children's panel and I was told if I needed any help just to let my social worker know. Just yesterday I had nothing at all for the kids and I called the social worker but it was just a blunt "no".' The children were placed on supervision (while staying at home), and Anita's fear that they would be removed combined with her anger and depression to make her refuse to open the door to social workers.

Carol protests that social workers were imposed upon her. She wrote, 'Because of my social circumstances and because of all my medication, I was put under the social worker in the hospital. I felt I never had the chance to be alone with my baby. I felt that decisions were being made above me because I was a single mother. It was hard for me to say no to officials because in the eyes of the Social Work Department that is you rejecting help and then they take you to the panels.' Carol's account displays the themes of resentment and fear. She resented that social workers made her have a homemaker, made her attend the nursery with her daughter, made her give up seeing a boyfriend. She resented that these impositions were not linked with any material help to the task of motherhood. She feared that her daughter would be taken from her. It was a realistic fear because her child did enter public care and social workers attempted to make it a permanent removal. Of course, the social workers were acting in what they saw as the best interests of the child, but they never seemed to engage Carol in a positive relationship, never seemed to be on the same side. Instead of a relationship there was procedure and conflict. This led to battle and eventually Carol did win her daughter back. But the cost of the battle was partly paid by Carol's daughter. Her comings and goings, her knowledge that her future was in doubt, must have increased her insecurities.

Denise also expressed some resentment and fear. She knew from her own childhood that children could be removed by social workers from their families. Sometimes this removal is justifiable and unavoidable, but it did not lessen Denise's worry that her children might be taken. After allowing other young women to look after her baby while she visited her mother, she was warned by a social worker that if she did it again 'they would ask for a supervision order on the baby'. Later another social worker visited after a health visitor reported a bruise on her boy. Denise showed her the bare boards on which he had fallen. She complained, 'We can't go out and leave the babies with anybody in case the social workers take them all off us.' She appeared to receive threats but not help.

Penny regarded social workers much more positively. At times she felt they should have enabled her to stay in the same flat. But mainly she saw social workers as a form of protection against her partner. They found her new accommodation and a solicitor. Penny particularly liked one social worker who clearly aimed to keep the children with Penny, who enabled her to obtain secondhand furniture, and who gave her some encouragement. Penny wrote with some pride that 'the social worker said it was marvellous how I managed the money'.

The different experiences of the writers reflect two strands of contemporary social work, sometimes entitled Protection and Prevention. During the 1970s and 1980s, social workers were criticized in a number of official reports for failing to prevent the abuse, even deaths, of certain children who had been left with their parents. In reaction, Social Services Departments and Social Work Departments shifted resources towards the protection and often removal of children and away from prevention (or family support as it was also called). The concentration on protection facilitated the rise of a harsher form of social work. Bill Jordan, probably the leading social work academic, observed that social work has 'become more coercive and restrictive' with staff checking behaviour, threatening to remove children in order to get compliance like agreeing to attend a centre for training or treatment, and denying parental access to their children.[11] As child protection dominated social work, the giving of emotional and practical support to parents to enable them to retain their children fell out of fashion. It did not disappear, but in terms of training, status and resources, it received less priority, and it appears that some children were removed from parents who could have retained their care given better support. Now there are signs that prevention is to make a come-back. Sir Herbert Laming, the Chief Inspector of the Social Services Inspectorate, stated in his report for 1996/97, that there were 'unsatisfactory services which do nothing to dispel the fears of families about what might happen as a result of SSD involvement' and asserted that 'Good child care practice begins by exploring ways in which families can be supported in their responsibilities for bringing up children.'[12]

The contributors to this book, as those at the receiving end, give their perspectives about social work. Clearly, controlling or macho social work did not help them to become better parents. Social workers who impose decisions, who use threats, who appear unsympathetic, provoke a fear and resentment which undermines people like Erica, Anita, Denise and Carol. Far more is achieved by those who form warm relationships, who offer practical support, and who convey that their first aim is to keep the family united. To repeat, sometimes children do have to be removed, but Erica's social worker showed that within a friendly yet professional relationship such a decision could be reached with the parents.

Some departments are returning to earlier experiments with community social work. This involves social work teams being located within areas of high social need, of being close to residents and also of participating with them in local activities. In Rotherham, a team on a neglected estate encouraged residents to form play schemes, women's groups and youth clubs. These activities brought isolated parents together and provided outlets for their children and so alleviated some local problems; the nearness of the social workers meant that needy parents came to them early before their difficulties became a crisis; the outcome was that numbers of children in care decreased while none were seriously abused.[13] In short, prevention and protection can go together. The words of the parents who have written in this book lend support to this kind of social work.

## The Christian church

Residents in inner-city areas will be aware of the importance of many different religious faiths. In Easterhouse, however, I know of no churches except Christian ones, and the contributors made mention only of them. This section, therefore, will concentrate on the Christian church and, in particular, on the Salvation Army because it was an important resource to the writers.

### The Easterhouse Salvation Army

Church attendance is notoriously low on council estates. Yet six of the contributors at some stage lived near to and had contact with the Easterhouse Corps of the Salvation Army. It was under the leadership of Captain Eric and Anne Buchanan. They are now retired, following the captain suffering a stroke, but they were the officers about whom the contributors write. It is useful to describe the Buchanans. They were not brought up as salvationists and did not enter its ministry until middle age. Consequently, they were not steeped in tradition. For most of their time in Easterhouse, they lived in rooms above two small halls, one for worship, one for social activities. In run down condition and with the windows covered with wire and boards, the building was sometimes known as 'the fortress'.

Captain Eric Buchanan was forceful, outspoken and devoted to Easterhouse. Three incidents reflect his approach.

On one occasion we had gone to Motherwell in the Sally's battered minibus when he noticed a Christian college. Marching in, he expressed disapproval of the expensive wood panelling and demanded to see the director. While I cringed in the background, the captain attacked with, 'You're a Christian yuppy. You should be working in somewhere like Easterhouse.' The director, a very gracious man, replied that Captain Buchanan was right and asked him to take some of his students on placements. The captain had to agree.

Easterhouse is a place of high unemployment. It is especially difficult for people with drinking problems to find jobs. On another occasion, Captain Buchanan determined to do something and set up a scheme whereby six men were paid to work in the grounds of Salvation Army establishments. Three of these subsequently found full-time posts as gardeners. One Christmas, the captain decided to take the six along with other volunteers from his huge secondhand store – Sally Army Seconds – for a meal. Unconventional as ever, he decided to go to a pub where he knew the manager. On arrival, the pub was being refitted with carpets. After the meal, with no alcohol, the captain had a word with the manager and we all walked out carrying the huge rolls of discarded carpet on our shoulders. Captain Buchanan was delighted. A cheap meal and good carpet for Easterhouse people.

On the third occasion, the hall was packed for the Christmas carol service. Mrs Buchanan was in the small hall dressing the children for the nativity play. The captain was leading with his usual gusto when he spotted a man entering the back door. He was obviously in need of help and the captain just walked out to assist him. The meeting came to a puzzled silence for several minutes before my wife, Annette, rose to organize community singing. His concern for that man was such that he forgot everything else.

Captain Buchanan considered the Christian gospel to be about material help and personal support to the needy. His outgoing manner and machine-gun-like questions did offend some people, yet others responded. Interestingly, a number of drug-abusers invited him in and trusted him. His concern for material needs did not mean, however, that he disregarded the call to people to make a personal relationship with God. The Sunday evening meeting was evangelical in nature and often ended with an invitation to kneel at the mercy seat. On such occasions, the captain would signal to a uniformed member to counsel the kneeling person. One Sunday

evening, he had preached passionately on the theme that
Jesus could solve any problem, and a number came
forward, including a youngster whom I knew. As the
uniformed staff were all allocated, the captain beckoned
me to help the boy. I came out and, in whispered tones,
asked him about the problem he wanted Jesus to solve.
He held up his wrist, pointed to his watch, and replied,
'It's broken, I want it to go again.' The miracle was
beyond me, but the captain roared with laughter and
searched for another watch. He believed in integrating
the material and the spiritual.

The writers had varying kinds of contacts with the
Salvation Army. As a child, Denise lived for a while with
her sister in a flat opposite the Sally building and
sometimes ventured into the clubs and meetings. Later, as
a teenage mother, she moved into a nearby flat where her
furniture consisted of one bed. Denise is reluctant to ask
for help but, as she already knew the captain and his wife,
she did approach them and obtained some secondhand
furniture.

Anita was a religious person who prayed and reflected.
Yet her misfortunes prompted doubts and deep questions.
She wrote, 'I think everybody doubts God when
something bad happens to them, it is because they feel
angry at a loved one being taken from them, and they
wonder if there really is a God.' Again, 'I don't think I am
a bad person or done anything really bad in this life, and
neither has any of my family. So why is God punishing
me? My brother Joe died and now my younger brother,
George, has been told he has cancer of the lungs. If
anything happens to George I could not cope with it

because I don't want to experience the pain and sorrow of losing another brother. Why does God let us suffer like this?'

Although a Catholic, Anita's depression and withdrawal meant she rarely attended church. However, in her poverty she would sometimes send her children with requests to the Salvation Army. Captain Buchanan responded with items ranging from a secondhand washing machine to food. When he delivered them he would talk with and pray with Anita.

In her narration, Penny tells how she was rehoused in Easterhouse. She continued, 'It was here I met Captain Buchanan of the Salvation Army. I remember him telling me to get rid of John and saying I would not have a good life with him. Alistair, who was about nine, started going to the clubs at the Salvation Army.' After being moved away, Penny returned to the district and wrote, 'It was very near the Salvation Army, so Alistair could go to the clubs again. He loved the clubs and it got him out of the house. He won a trophy for darts. He was over the moon about that and I was really proud of him... I started going to the Salvation Army. I got on great with Captain Buchanan and I enjoyed meeting different people.' With her partner spending money on drugs, Penny sometimes had to ask Captain Buchanan for 'food and clothes' but, she added, 'I used to get embarrassed about asking.'

Carol first approached the Salvation Army when her brother moved to Easterhouse. She wrote as follows:

I went along to the Salvation Army to get some secondhand furniture for him. It was there I met

Captain Buchanan. I could hardly believe him. In his old, baggy pullover, if it wasn't for his Salvation Army cap you would have thought he had come in looking for somewhere to stay. He was always rushing around for people. He was a bit like myself, he thought for others not for himself.

I started going to the services on a Sunday. The Social Work Department was getting really heavy with me and I was looking for someone to turn to apart from my dad. I was so mixed up and I wanted to test myself, 'Do I believe or not believe?' and if I did believe I wanted to know why all these things were happening to me. I got my daughter christened at the Sally. I started helping the captain at a Tuesday lunch club which he started for men, mostly alcoholics. I enjoyed that. When I saw the look on some of the guys' faces when I gave them mince and tatties, it made me realize how lucky I was... I enjoyed the services at the Sally and looked forward to them. I met friends there like the Thompsons and people who never held ill feelings against you. They always wanted to help, they gave me time and explained things. The Social Work Department had taken away all my confidence. At times I could not talk. I would just break down. I started to believe in God for selfish reasons at first. He was the only one who I could talk to and did not say bad things to me. God listened and gave me strength.

Erica turned to the Salvation Army at a time when her partner was drinking heavily. She wrote:

I needed help too, so I started to attend the Salvation Army. It was the best thing I had done in a long time. At first it was just me and the kids going, then I talked Ivor into coming with me to see what it was like and he liked it. The Salvation Army meant the world to me. The holidays at Butlins – and we never went on holidays before. The kids going to the Sunday School. Christmas Day at the Sally was great. I was in the women's choir which Annette led. I never missed a Sunday service. Captain and Mrs Buchanan were a part of our life and they still are even though they have retired. I always remember the captain's bushy eyebrows. It helped me to believe in God. It took me a long time to accept. I do believe although sometimes I doubt. I think, if there is a God why have all these things happened to me, why hasn't he prevented them? But it is not his fault that these things happen.

From the perceptions of the writers, and from my own involvement with them, it is clear that the Salvation Army was relevant to them in the following ways.

*Counselling.* Both Captain Eric and Anne Buchanan spent time with individuals. Captain Buchanan was often forthright in his advice and actions and could be incensed when women and children were badly treated. I recall one occasion when Penny's partner both kept her short of money and slapped her around. The captain was all for getting some of his heavies – reformed alcoholics – to give him a beating. He calmed down and told the partner he would report him to the police. It was a kind of righteous anger that flared up at bullying and social injustice. At other times, he melted into a quieter mood and would talk calmly, particularly with Carol, Erica and Penny, and inevitably end with a prayer. Anne Buchanan gave more time to chatting, listening and comforting. She was a kind of mother figure with whom women found it easy to discuss personal matters.

*Friendships.* The Salvation Army meetings invariably ended with cups of tea and time for talk. At these, new worshippers, often troubled and isolated people, made new acquaintances which sometimes blossomed into friendships. Erica appreciated being a member of the small women's group which sang on special occasions. Carol found a role at the lunches where she was part of a team which prepared and served food to very needy men. Penny would often drop in for a chat with others. These and other attenders formed a kind of fellowship who not only came to the regular meetings but also enjoyed eating together at the Easter breakfast, the harvest dinner and the Christmas lunch. Friendships made at the Sally would often be continued outside with visits to each others' homes. They felt united around the focus of their church.

*Practical help.* All the writers who mentioned the Salvation Army referred to receiving material help. Usually it was secondhand furniture for which they paid a modest price. Sometimes it was clothing and bedding purchased at one of the jumble sales. For some, the Sally was the source of their only holiday. These practical services were essential to people with very low incomes. They could also be social occasions. Visits to the furniture store often meant seeing friends or a chance for a talk with Mrs Buchanan. The jumble sales included the occasion for a cup of tea and a cake. I first met Carol at one of the sales. The annual holiday at Butlins enabled whole families to go away together. In fact, the holiday was so good that it unofficially expanded. One year Captain Buchanan was puzzled when more people got off the coach on its return than when it left seven days before. It appeared that once settled in their chalets, some of the holidaymakers had invited friends to enter Butlins on a day pass and then stay with them for the rest of the week.

*The children's clubs.* The Sally held a Sunday School; the Covenanters, a Christian group for older children; and two youth clubs (after the Buchanans retired the clubs were transferred to FARE). The clubs could be chaotic and crowded. The captain ran a café and tried to keep order. Volunteers such as myself tried to organize team games amidst the table tennis, snooker and craft activities. Sometimes, the space became even smaller as the captain's men arrived after the closure of the store and had to unload furniture or food. On sunny summer evenings, Captain Buchanan organized transport to take the junior children to Drumpelier Park. Occasionally on a Saturday, Anne Buchanan arranged for them to attend larger events run by the Salvation Army. Denise, when a child, Bill, and the children of Erica, Penny, Anita and Carol, were among the many who came. The clubs simply gave the kids somewhere to go. For parents with large families and overcrowded rooms, it also afforded a twice-a-week respite.

*Finding God.* Many people came to the jumble sales,

Sally Seconds, the holidays, without wanting any spiritual involvement. Captain and Mrs Buchanan considered that to help their material wants was a Christian service. But they made no secret of their belief that all people had a need to find the fatherhood of God, the forgiveness of Jesus Christ, and the power of the Holy Spirit. It was at the Sally that Erica and Carol did find strength and comfort in making a spiritual commitment. Anita prayed daily and tried to live a Christian life despite overwhelming difficulties. Young Bill, in the midst of a teenage life which entailed unemployment and the pressures of drugs and crime, could state, 'Christianity makes me a bit stronger.' These writers, and others who attended the Sally, demonstrated that Christianity was for them just as much as for the affluent, that they could worship God in the battered and draughty Sally hall just as much as those in the grandest cathedral.

Easterhouse Salvation Army under the leadership of the Buchanans should not be held up as an exemplary church. Far from it. Some residents found the captain too abrasive and would not put a foot across the door. Christians who attended, but who were not Salvationists, could feel uneasy with the uniforms and hierarchical ranking system in the Salvation Army. Numbers at the Sunday meetings fluctuated between a crowded hall and a handful. The social activities did not please all participants. Some of the Butlins' holidaymakers complained about rowdy behaviour and did not want to go again. The clubs were not well prepared and their equipment was inadequate. As the children grew older, it was clear that a number left as they became embarrassed by their association with what other youngsters nicknamed 'The Starvation Army'. Not least, the giving out of material goods had overtones of Victorian charity. Penny wrote about how awkward she felt when asking for help. Once, when she was penniless, she sent her son to ask for food which the captain provided. The boy told me how he disliked doing this and explained, 'I felt like a beggar.' To be fair, Captain Buchanan was aware of such feelings and disliked his charity role – hence the setting-up of a store where people purchased furniture at modest prices. He was angry with a society which resulted in some families being without food and money at weekends. None the less, when they came to his door, he felt he had to provide something. For all its limitations, the Easterhouse Sally did attract numbers of low-incomed residents and, as some of the contributors revealed, it did have a significance for them.

## Churches in deprived areas

As put forward in Part 1 of this book, I regard equality as a corollary of Christianity. I believe that God intended the material and social advantages of his world – along with its responsibilities – to be available to all. Similarly, I believe that he wants all people to enter into a personal relationship with himself. In Britain, churchgoing is not high anywhere, but a survey made in 1995 shows it to be highest in places like East Devon, Exeter, Oxford and Bournemouth and lowest in places like Hackney, Newham and Newcastle upon Tyne.[14] Christians tend to be concentrated in more prosperous locations and to be thin on the ground in the poorer ones. There are exceptions. In the inner cities, a few churches, especially charismatic fellowships, are growing. But, in general, churches in socially deprived areas, particularly in council estates, are not drawing in local residents. It follows that populations of these areas have less chance of hearing the good news of Christianity. Poor people thus face a spiritual inequality. I do not have the answers. But drawing both upon over twenty years' experience in such areas and upon the writings of my friends, I wish to suggest a few indicators of how churches can be relevant. Much depends on the church's leadership style, neighbourhood style, helpers' style and outsiders' style.

*Leadership style,* be it by vicars, priests, pastors, captains or lay persons, is crucial. Almost essential is that they should be residents of, not commuters into, the areas. Only by living there do they identify with local people, by using the same shops, waiting for the same buses, meeting their kids at the same schools. Only by living there do they take on the same disadvantages, be it having their car vandalized or not having a garden. Only by living there can they be constantly available to needy people. And only by living there can they benefit from the friendliness and cheerfulness of neighbours.

It is an advantage if leaders have local roots and so readily and easily identify with local culture, its language, its jokes, its values. The Buchanans were Glaswegians, although the captain was born in Northern Ireland as his father's Scottish regiment was stationed there at the time. By contrast, when I first came to Easterhouse a local punter gruffly informed me, 'We don't like English people here – but it's better than coming from Edinburgh.' Others admitted that at least I had the good sense to marry a Glaswegian. Glaswegians are suspicious of outsiders, but it can be overcome. My arrival coincided with the start of the soap opera *Eastenders*, and kids used to mimic my nasal tones and ask what it was like in Albert Square. The point was that they liked *Eastenders* and it made for common ground. The response should not be to try to speak the local accent. This is false and appears ridiculous. Far better to acknowledge differences and, sometimes, to joke about them. I like to claim that West Ham United are far better than Celtic and Rangers, and neighbours have reacted by watching for the West Ham results and then often laughing at me. More important, incomers can enter into local life, participate in local campaigns – such as stopping the closure of the school – join a local institution be it football team, political party or pub. The barriers are then lowered.

Probably the most important way of gaining acceptance is by staying long-term. Members of deprived areas can be cynical about middle-class professionals who move in, leave after a year or so and then use the experience as a career step in social work or for collecting data for a thesis. I believe that church leaders should commit themselves for at least a decade. As the years go by so long-standing residents will perceive them as having a genuine interest in them and their neighbourhood. Staying long-term brings other advantages. Leaders will find that they grow with local families; that is they see them in changing times. They find that it is easier to cope with aggressive teenagers when they have known them as young children. Further, over the years they will become well-known figures: they will be pointed out as the priest who married us, the minister who christened our children, the pastor who buried our dad, the youth club leader who took us on holidays. Then when needy families move into the area, neighbours will be prepared to tell them that these leaders can be approached with confidence.

Living locally for a long period will establish leaders in the neighbourhood. They will have established a certain style. This is essential but not sufficient. Leaders will almost certainly be approached by individuals with personal problems which require skilled handling. Often the technical nature of the help required is beyond them but, at least, they should know where to refer them and perhaps accompany them to Citizens Advice Bureaux, to lawyers, to social workers, and so on. However, church leaders can also become skilled in certain specialisms. They can become experienced in attending children's hearings (in Scotland) or youth courts, in negotiating with debt collectors, in advising on basic welfare rights matters, in negotiating with council officials, particularly those from housing. Residents will then turn to leaders both because they have won their trust as long-term neighbours and also because they are known as possessing certain skills. This is the kind of leadership style which is valued and wanted in deprived areas.

This leadership style should be combined with a *church neighbourhood style*. Evangelical churchgoers will be familiar with sermons about the dangers of worldliness. Some churches have almost withdrawn from contact with their communities and have taken on a siege mentality in which the church buildings become castles with the drawbridges lowered just for Sunday meetings and mid-week prayer gatherings. If I understand the life of Christ aright, then he was fully immersed in the world without succumbing to the worldly values of selfishness and greed. Within the context of deprived areas, the church's role must be to reach out to the material and social needs of residents on the grounds that God is concerned about these needs. At times, Christians will feel compelled to give money and food directly to those who are in desperate straits. This must be done sensitively and confidentially in order to minimize the charity handout approach which can demean recipients. Far better, however, if churches as agencies and Christians as individuals participate in neighbourhood co-operative ventures which make goods available in ways which uphold human dignity. A furniture store can involve local people in collecting and repairing goods which are then sold not given. A food co-operative can entail members buying at markets and then selling cheaply to each other: the North Easterhouse Food Co-op was able to sell bread at 27p a loaf as against 50p on the vans. Credit unions draw in low-incomed residents who save together and then lend out at low interest rates. These organizations thus meet practical needs and help to alleviate poverty but they do so by stimulating members of the neighbourhoods to do it for themselves. Churches in deprived areas are important to such initiatives for often they possess the only halls from which they can operate and possess the only minibuses which can move furniture or collect food. The churches may choose to organize such projects themselves or individual Christians may join others in projects which belong to the neighbourhoods. Either way, Christians are making a contribution to their neighbourhood.

It was said that church leaders will be drawn into giving personal help, often skilled help, to individuals. Sometimes these relationships are the only way to help because the person in need requires a confidential one-to-one relationship. Undoubtedly, the Christian leader who can listen with empathy and advise with sensitivity is an enormous asset in locations where people can be almost destroyed with financial, emotional and physical anxieties. The trouble is that the leader can support so many individuals that they themselves become overburdened and worn out. The church requires a *collective helping style*. As a leader, I took some satisfaction in encouraging residents to be committee members, volunteers at the youth clubs, helpers at the holidays. Unfortunately, I had a big plank called 'I am indispensable' in my eye which blinded me to their abilities as counsellors. Then I was confined to home for a long period following an operation. Others took over my role and did it just as well if not better. This is not to say that any person can do so. It is to say that the skills and principles of counselling are not restricted to just one person.

In like manner a church can develop small teams who share out support to individuals. But help can also be offered in a group setting. In Australia, Jane Thomson made a detailed study of a neighbourhood project which employed, part-time, local women as family aides. They were all mothers who had themselves overcome family and financial problems. After some basic in-service training, they formed a group with other women who had been referred to the project because of severe financial and parenting difficulties which were considered to put their children at risk. They met regularly together, discussed problem-solving such as how to negotiate with officials, went out as a social group, arranged practical services like baby-minding. The outcomes were successful with none of the mothers slipping into child neglect or abuse. Thomson attributes the success partly to the mothers being able to identify easily with persons from their own backgrounds and partly to the fact that they saw that improvement was possible. Indeed, it appears that this help was more useful than that given by professional workers whom Thomson also studied.[15]

If they had been at the Salvation Army at the same time, I could envisage Carol, Penny and Erica acting together to help other parents with problems like their own. Churches in the inner cities and council estates may have few attenders and they may be very similar to these women. Yet these are the very people who, acting collectively, could be a source of strength to others. They could do the Christian service of helping others with their material, social and family problems. And also with their spiritual needs. Interestingly, Thomson in her secular investigation and Wilkinson in his treatise on equality note that the people they studied were also seeking a meaning to life. Professor Wilkinson, while advocating greater material equality, yet observes, 'We are not merely

economic beings, with material needs, motivated by
material gain...Vitally important is the way in which we
fit into a wider structure of meaning.'[16] Collective help
by low-incomed Christians to residents similar to
themselves could also lead to insights about meaning,
about the Christian understanding of life.

Churches in deprived areas may often feel isolated and
cut off from other churches. Sometimes I visit prosperous
churches with their wood panelling, sophisticated
electronic equipment and car parks jammed with space
wagons – at which I cast envious looks. They seem in a
different world from the boarded-up windows and the
old-fashioned foot organ in inner-city and estate
churches, where only a handful of members have jobs and
even fewer have cars. Yet they are all a part of the body of
Christ. They are all part of the one church universal. The
question then arises, how can the prosperous churches
help the poor ones. What is the appropriate *outsider style*?

Elsewhere I have suggested that churches should move
their administrative centres, their publishing houses, their
training colleges into deprived areas. Such moves would
create jobs in places of high unemployment and would be
a means of injecting cash into run-down economies.[17]
Less radically, outside churches can enter into
partnerships with those inside the inner cities and estates.
The richer churches could offer practical help. I know of
one such church which installed a burglar alarm into an
estate church which was plagued by break-ins. The alarm,
which was connected to the police station, greatly
reduced the burglaries. But it has to be a genuine
partnership with members from the materially poorer

churches making a return, for instance, in the form of organizing an outing for the elderly folk or running a play-day for the children of the outside churches.

Lastly, should Christians from outside deliberately choose to move into deprived zones? In the USA, Robert Lupton urges Christians from suburban areas to 'relocate' to the inner city and explains that Jesus himself dwelt mainly with poor people. Lupton's major concern is to revive local churches. He adds that the incomers will also bring in new leaders and will improve the economy of the area.[18]

I share Lupton's concern and welcome Christians who come to stay. However, I consider that incoming Christians must proceed with caution and humility. It is false if they present themselves as missionaries who bring God in from outside. God is already there in needy areas. Those coming in simply join some of God's people, often few in number, who have lived there for years and know more about the area than the newcomers ever will. Further, whatever their qualifications and abilities, they must be prepared to learn from resident Christians. Erica is too modest to write herself, but I recall one Sunday when she and her husband had just 15p left and their kids were pestering them to spend it on sweets from the van. They refused. That evening at the Salvation Army, she put it all in the collection. It was the modern widow's mite. I had to learn that her giving was sacrificial giving. The fiver I put in was not. Christian newcomers can strengthen local churches. But they must come in the style set down by Jesus, the *servant style*. This does not entail being servile or weak, for Jesus was far from that. It does mean a readiness not to impose upon others but rather to offer to join with them in fellowship and action.

Churches in areas characterized by unemployment, poverty, lack of amenities, neglect by statutory and commercial forces, do have disadvantages not carried by those in prosperous places. In order to express the whole gospel, they require a distinctive leadership style, a church neighbourhood style, a members' collective helping style, and partnership expressed in outsider style. This all comes together in servant style which can make the church relevant by being a servant to God and to the community.

## What we want

I used to have on my bookshelf a book written in the 1920s by trade union activists. It was called *What We Want and Why*. Written by working-class people, immersed in the struggle for better work and living conditions, it made powerful reading. In like manner, the contributors to this book have their views on what they want and why.

This is not to say they are wholly dissatisfied with the present. Without exception, they praise local agencies and churches. Cynthia explains that for her family the prospect of flitting from the inner city to Easterhouse was seen as going to the new Jerusalem. And, indeed, they rejoiced that their new flat had an inside toilet and bath, a front and back door, and a garden. Carol writes appreciatively about neighbours, teachers, the janny at the primary school, and she has no wish to move from

Easterhouse. Bill said that he had got used to the place and enjoyed the clubs. Penny was made to leave Easterhouse but was pleased to return. Erica left to protect her children from racial abuse but missed the place. Anita was the one most anxious to move out in order to remove her children from the threat of drug abuse. Paradoxically, she also writes lovingly about her son who is a heroin addict. She stated, 'My heart aches for my son Peter. But he is a tower of strength to me.'

Peter with his demands for money created much trouble, but he was a major source of personal comfort and of looking after the younger children. Anita continued, 'To me he is the best son a mother could have.' Anita is making an important point, that drug abusers are human beings who have positive aspects. Similarly, the contributors – unlike outsiders who just dwell upon the negative aspects of Easterhouse – are revealing their mixed feelings for Easterhouse. This is what Paul Henderson calls 'counter-information' which only local residents can supply.[19] They produce a more balanced viewpoint, one that sees Easterhouse as having positives and negatives, advantages and disadvantages.

But disadvantages there are. Cynthia explained that from the start Easterhouse lacked facilities with a lack of adequate shops, leisure amenities and recreational facilities. She also regretted that the flats of the New Jerusalem were neglected so leading to problems of damp and decay. Carol complained about the continuation of gang-fighting and the growing violence associated with drug abuse. She explained, 'Drugs is a problem. The sad thing is that many druggies turn to stealing to pay for it...

Just last week there was a murder, a nineteen-year-old boy.' Carol pinpointed unemployment saying, 'There are no jobs here,' and regretted that youngsters applying for posts outside were advised to hide the fact that they came from Easterhouse. She acknowledged that FARE provided youth facilities in one district but said that there were none near her family. She added, 'The sports centre is quite expensive and it is in the centre where a lot of kids do not go in case they get jumped.' Denise and Bill, the youngest contributors, were also worried about crime and drug abuse. Denise said, 'We can't go outside the door at night because there are junkies' needles lying about.' Bill was angry about the lack of jobs. He went on one training scheme, but 'That was a year and a half ago and I have been on the broo ever since. I have been trying to get jobs but they keep on saying there are no vacancies or "we will get in touch," but I never hear.' Anita associated Easterhouse with the traumatic death of her husband and considered that its disadvantages weighed upon her children. She recorded, 'I desperately want away from this place for my kids' sake and to try and give them a better life.'

The contributors thus had differing views about Easterhouse. This is not surprising, for Easterhouse is a large place with parts which have good housing and parts which don't, with areas which have youth amenities and those which don't, with streets which are comparatively safe from crime and drug abuse and those which have them to the brim. But the contributors were all agreed that improvements were essential. They wanted a better future.

## What they want

So what do the contributors want? First, all want
something better for their children. Penny desires to be
able to bring up her children without fear and want.
Erica put it, 'I hope my children have a better future.'
Anita writes, 'They are lovely kids and intelligent and I
would dearly love to see them make something of
themselves.' Significantly, all want secure and united
families, with lives free from drugs and trouble and with
hope for the future. Indeed, all the writers value family
life. Their wishes reinforce a point made earlier. These
low-income residents of a deprived area are not an
underclass intent on destroying traditional family unity.
Their hopes, aspirations and values are in common with
those of most other citizens. But if these aims are to be
achieved they require different social conditions.

Second, they want relief from poverty. As Erica
explained, 'I don't like the poverty, I don't like the kids
coming home and asking for something I can't give
them.' Anita reflected, 'Some people say that money is the
root of all evil. But if I just had enough to help my kids,
it would be like a gift from heaven. It can't be evil if you
put it to good use and see the happiness in the kids' faces
even if it is just a little thing they have always wanted.'

Third, jobs. The younger writers wanted job
opportunities. Denise dreamt, 'In the future, when the
weans are grown up, I'd like to have a job so I can get out
of the house. I'd like to work in a hospital.' Bill recorded,
'In the future, I would like to see my mum more happy,
and my brothers and sisters. I'd like to settle down and get

a good job and a good place to live.' These writers are not fools. They recognize that jobs are crucial as an avenue out of poverty. Noticeably, the two contributors who now have the most stable and secure lives – Cynthia and Carol – had fathers who were in employment and husbands who have known employment. By contrast, the husband of Erica and the partners of Penny and Denise were long-term unemployed. Anita's husband had been out of work, and she believes that his suicide was linked with depression about his unemployment. Further, her sons lacked jobs. From what they wrote and from what I know of these families, it is almost certain that the lack of satisfying jobs and the boredom of years on the dole was a pressure that made them vulnerable to drink, drugs and crime. With the exception of Penny's partner, it is to their credit that – with the support of their loved ones – they did remain part of their families. But their lives and that of their families will be vastly improved if jobs become available.

Fourth, more local projects. Cynthia glows with the success of the housing co-operative and sees it as a model for the future. She confidently predicts, 'as far as I am concerned, "things can only get better"'. Carol asserts that the government should take action to improve the job situation in Easterhouse and adds, 'But we must act as well. Easterhouse has a bad reputation for drugs, violence, deprivation. People should be able to walk through their own scheme instead of getting stabbed. We must act because the community needs to be for each other.' Carol can draw upon her own involvement in neighbourhood projects to show that local action can improve circumstances. However, she wants more action particularly in two directions. She considers that the problems of drug abuse should be taken more seriously, with children given more education about the dangers and with more counselling services available to addicts. Further, she argues that 'Sports centres and community centres need to be in each area so that they are for each community.' She believes that youth amenities within each neighbourhood would be of more use than larger ones placed in the centre of Easterhouse. In recognizing the existence of territorial boundaries which some youngsters will not cross, Carol illustrates how much better future plans would be if made by experienced insiders rather than by expert outsiders.

**Three policy proposals**

I live in Easterhouse, but I am not the same as the seven people who have written the middle and most important section of this book. My wife and I have chosen to live here: we have purchased our flat and, we are free to move away – if we could ever sell our flat, that is! I spend the bulk of my time in the neighbourhood, but my income comes from teaching at a university for half a day a week and writing occasional articles and books. I therefore have links with both the inside and outside worlds. From the inside, I want to draw upon what I know about the contributors, what they write about themselves, and what they wish for the future, in order to make three policy proposals. I present these to the outside world of politicians, academics and those who write about social policy. They apply to reform at national, local government and neighbourhood levels

At *national government level,* there is a strong case for increased rates of income support. The Labour Government has indicated that it intends to tackle poverty by a 'welfare to work' programme. In regard to lone mothers, it intends to abolish the lone parent premium and the one parent premium for new claimants in 1998. Instead, lone parents will be encouraged to take paid employment. The government will not raise income support levels except to keep them in line with inflation. It has set up a Social Exclusion Unit – social exclusion being a new polite term for poverty – under the minister without portfolio, Peter Mandelson. At a lecture given at its inception, Mandelson indicated that a pound a week extra would do little good for those on income support and underlined that the way ahead was to equip people for the jobs market.[20]

As the young contributors indicated, new jobs with reasonable wages are required. But it is hard to see how lone parents, like Anita and Penny, could take on employment. Anita is struggling to keep together a family which includes a drug abuser and a son who has problems attending school. Penny frequently moves her family in order to hide from her former partner. Carol, Denise and Erica have come through traumatic experiences to the point where they are coping with their children. To push them into jobs would undermine their role as parent. From knowing them over the years, my view is that they deserve credit for preserving their family units and avoiding their children having to enter permanent and expensive long-term public care. The best way by which the state could enable them to continue in their valuable parenting would be to increase income support. This is not the place to debate just what levels should be set. It is enough to refer to the research published by the Rowntree Foundation which shows that income support allowances for children are way below their needs[21] and to lend support to the case put forward by Professor Ruth Lister, former director of the Child Poverty Action Group, that social security benefits should 'provide beneficiaries with an income sufficient to enable them to participate in society as full citizens'.[22] It must be added that even a small increase above inflation would help. An extra few pounds a week for each member of the family means very little to a cabinet minister on a salary of £100,000 a year plus expenses. Erica's detailed budget shows that, for people on income support, it could mean a proper meal, the central heating on for a few hours, the kids going on a school treat.

The graphic accounts by the contributors show that life under the present system of social security meant real hardship compounded by a sense of powerlessness and monotony. Their weekly incomes had been decreased by the introduction of social fund loans which replaced single payment grants for essential domestic items. The contributors show that in order to obtain, say, an official loan for a cooker, they face the prospect of weekly deductions which then mean they have to cut down the amounts spent on food. A cooker or food? My recommendation is for the abolition of loans and a return to grants to claimants who show that their cooker, fridge, bed, or the like, is no longer usable. When single-payment grants were abolished they were costing the government about £200 million. Put that against the £750 million which the government is setting aside for the prestigious Greenwich Millennium Dome and it does not seem such a large amount.

At *local government level*, Social Services Departments and Social Work Departments should give priority to community social work. The contributors displayed mixed feelings towards social workers. They reacted badly to heavy-handed approaches and positively to social workers who treated them with empathy and respect. Community social work involves staff being located within areas of high social need, and where they can participate with residents in improving local services. The physical and social closeness promotes both knowledge of and respect for each other. The outcome is that parents who are having childcare difficulties then tend to regard social workers not as enemy officials who want to remove their children but as professional friends who want to help them cope adequately with them.

At *neighbourhood level*, voluntary projects require the means to flourish. Interestingly, none of the writers mentioned national voluntary societies. But all spoke about locally controlled neighbourhood groups which were valued because staff were available and because residents – with Cynthia and Carol being examples – can benefit by making a contribution themselves. In a study of neighbourhood groups, I point out that they have over two million participants who help to run credit unions, food co-ops, youth clubs, day care facilities for small children, holidays for all ages and so on.[23] For all their attributes, neighbourhood groups have two major limitations. They are not spread evenly over the country, not even across deprived areas. If Erica had had access to one as a youngster, she might well have related with a trustworthy adult to whom she could have turned for protection from the terrible things that were happening to her. As Penny has moved around, she has frequently phoned the project in Easterhouse because she could find nothing like it in her latest neighbourhood. This lack of coverage probably connects with the other limitation. Neighbourhood groups have no secure source of funding. Central government will finance the large national voluntary societies but not local ones. Local authorities do grant aid to some neighbourhood groups but, when cuts are made, they are first to suffer. The unhappy outcome is that top local authority officials – whose own annual salaries amount to more than the total income of small projects – then recommend the chop for services to the poorest citizens. A number of charitable trusts are sympathetic to neighbourhood groups, but their funds are limited. Neighbourhood groups are sometimes advised to seek sponsorship from local industry or to set up profit-making enterprises in order to be self-sufficient. The advice tends to come from those who do not live on peripheral estates where there are few local firms and where there is no market for enterprises. Low-incomed residents thus find themselves participating, not only as volunteers to organize services, but also as desperate fundraisers running bingo, raffles and sponsored walks.

For lack of money, neighbourhood groups cannot fulfill their potential and some even have to close.

In recent years, I have put forward a proposal for a government-financed National Neighbourhood Fund. It would distribute money to, say, 250 Neighbourhood Trusts covering the most socially deprived areas. The members of each trust would be *elected* from their areas and they – not appointed quangos – would allocate funds to neighbourhood projects which are genuinely under local control. The outcomes would be five-fold.

First, financial security for existing groups and the start of new ones. The contributors' stories indicate that poor citizens are often shunted around from one estate to another. An increase in neighbourhood groups would mean that they would always have access to a local service.

Second, the services provided would not abolish poverty, but they would improve the quality of life for the bottom 30 per cent of the population.

Third, more residents would be involved and so gain the feelings of satisfaction recorded by Cynthia and Carol.

Fourth, neighbourhood groups would employ more local people in the youth clubs, credit unions, food co-ops and so on. Unemployment would be reduced. Moreover, unlike statutory professionals who tend to commute into disadvantaged areas but spend their salaries elsewhere, these workers would buy locally and so give a boost to the neighbourhood economy.

Fifth, strengthened by their collective participation, residents could write more, publish more, and persuade the media that people like themselves are capable of contributing to national debates.

These policy proposals to increase income support, to extend community social work and to establish a National Neighbourhood Fund are not part of government policy. In making them I draw heavily upon the words and experiences of people at the hard end. By contrast, government policymakers rely upon advisers and members of think-tanks who are more likely to have had experience of Oxbridge than council estates, who are more likely to be privileged than deprived. Yet the same government says 'We are about building a fairer society... where every family can feel it has a stake in society.'[24] The kind of individuals who have contributed to this book represent families which do not have a fair stake in society. Not one word has been written by anyone with an income above the average wage, not one sentence by anyone who lives in a comfortable suburb. More important, most of the contributors have existed in poverty and dreadful housing conditions. If the government really wants to give them a greater stake in society then it should listen less to the privileged and more to the deprived. It should have faith in the poor.

No doubt, the policy proposals will be met with the response that the country cannot afford more public expenditure. From where is the money to come? The answer is straightforward. From a progressive income tax system. A recent study by the Institute for Fiscal Studies concluded that, over the last twenty years, the richest 10 per cent of the population gained massively to the loss of the bottom 10 per cent. By 1995, the top 10 per cent enjoyed average incomes (after tax) of £23,600 a year while the bottom 10 per cent had £5,720.[25] The increasing inequality is partly explained by changes in the tax system which the Conservative governments manipulated to favour the affluent to the detriment of the poor. My plea is that the present Labour government should place heavier taxes on the wealthy in order to pursue the three policies. As I have explained elsewhere, higher income tax does not necessarily remove the incentive to work hard, while the relief of poverty, the promotion of preventative social work, and the expansion of neighbourhood groups are a form of social and economic investment which create a stronger society.[26]

The present government will reply that it was not elected on a manifesto to increase taxation. When I voted, as a Labour Party member for thirty-five years, I wanted a taxation system which took from the wealthy to give to the poor. Polls indicated that a sizeable proportion of the population thought likewise. But if the present government regards this as a stumbling-block then I argue that the tackling of poverty is so important that it should go to the country again with a different, more radical manifesto, one that reflects the interests of what Hutton calls the bottom 30 per cent rather than the interests of the stock exchange and the City of London.

### 'Hundreds of millionaires but thousands living in poverty'

Anita observed, 'My kids don't stand a chance. I don't think it is fair. There are hundreds of millionaires in this world but thousands living in poverty. When I pray at night, I ask why one person is better off than others and why God put us on the earth. Certainly it cannot be to make one person better than others, but that is the way it is just now – the rich and the poor. Why, as we are all equal?' Erica concluded her contribution by pointing out that she was still paying for last year's Christmas presents and that sometimes she had to borrow to eat. She wrote, 'I don't think I have much time for politics... But I do think everyone should be equal.'

The writers are correct to put their finger on inequality. It is not just that they are poor but that their low incomes are within a society where many have enormous incomes; they are in a society with a government reluctant to reduce substantially the income differences between the rich and the poor. While writing the last part of this book I have cut out reports from newspapers and put them against some of the experiences of the Easterhouse residents.

'The three men walked into Le Gavroche at 8pm. Five hours later their bill for a three-course dinner came to £13,091.20... Silvano Giraldin, general manager of the Michelin two-star restaurant in Mayfair, central London, said: "I am sure this new record will be broken shortly. There are many more people who can afford it these days."'[27]

*My morning starts by getting the children up for school. They don't eat in the morning before they go, but I make sure they have a packet of crisps for their tuck, although I have got to either ask the van or borrow for it.*

The government's social security minister launched The Centre for Analysis of Social Exclusion at the London School of Economics funded with a £2 million grant from public money. The minister 'supported Howard Glennerster LSE professor of social policy', who was opposed to government money being used to make 'across-the-board benefit increases which do not make the poor very much better off'.[28]

*Gilbert is off school at the moment because he needs new shoes and that is £10. I can't afford them just now.*

Graduates joining investment banks can expect, by their twenties, £160,000 a year. 'The offices of Morgan Stanley, a US-based bank which employs 2,600 people at Canary Wharf, have the atmosphere of an American five-star hotel. The noiseless corridors are deeply carpeted and lined with works of art...There are two fitness suites, a beauty salon, a dance studio and a dry cleaner.'[29]

*I get £57 a fortnight, of which I give mum £30. So I get about £18 a week. You can't do much with that.*

Cabinet ministers were divided as to whether they should accept huge pay rises to take them to over £100,000 a year. The *Daily Mail* pointed out that nearly all were already numbered amongst the affluent and privileged. Of Harriet Harman, the Minister for Social Security, who was determined to cut benefits to one-parent families, it pointed out that her salary would rise to £103,860, that she lived in a 'rambling old house in South London which she has shared with her union leader Jack Dromey since the eighties. Could be worth up to £200,000... Dromey's salary is estimated at... about £35,000. Her late father was a Harley Street doctor and her mother a lawyer. Lady Longford is her aunt.'[30]

*I ended up in the council's homeless unit. We were there for seven months. It was tough. Alistair was a few months old and the hostel was cold. It was only bed and breakfast so you had to stay out for your lunch and tea. I walked about looking in shops. Sometimes I felt like taking my own life but I had to think of my son.*

'Visitors seeking an audience with Peter Mandelson will be able to wait in awesome splendour from next week thanks to a £15,703 refurbishment paid for by the taxpayer. The 18th century ante-room to Mr Mandelson's chamber has been restored to its former glory so that guests can sit in squashy armchairs and rest their feet on thick pile carpets before being ushered into his presence.'[31]

*I have been very excited since Sunday... There are private landlords with furnished rooms in safe places and you have to put down a deposit. My friend suggested we write to a trust to try and get the deposit. If he can help us move away he will be giving four children a chance in life. It ended in disappointment. We discovered that the rents are above what we would get from housing benefit. The landlords do not want people like me.*

'Parents spend nearly £500 on each child to keep them entertained over the summer holidays, says a report today by Switch... The biggest bill is the annual holiday – an average of £950 for a family of four – £227 for each child. Summer school costs about £51, holiday clothes £50, trips to theme parks £28, zoos £17 and watching the latest films £13.'[32]

*I am stuck in most of the time... We wash them [the children] and put them to bed about seven o'clock. Then we sit on the bed and watch telly, which saves putting the fire on.*

*Occasionally we go to bingo. We can't go outside the door at night because there are junkies' needles lying about.*

'Boys' clothes from Jigsaw branches nationwide. Leather jacket, £325; poplin shirt £49.95; corduroy trousers £59.95; corduroy suit £245.'[33]

*I find it very hard to live on the money. For the kids' clothes I go to charity shops. I can't afford to go into proper shops like Poundstretchers or British Home Stores.*

Sir Christopher Ball, former bursar at Lincoln College, Oxford, admitted that 'academic bursars have been hoodwinking governments for the past 20 years... to secure excessive annual increases in the college fee, a special subsidy to support the Oxbridge tutorial system worth £35 million a year'.[34]

*But there are not many amenities for them (the young people)... The government should put money into Easterhouse because others won't.*

The words of the contributors and the pages of newspapers act as a mirror which reflects the enormous inequalities in Britain. The inequalities are wrong because they impose on the disadvantaged a social suffering which is both unnecessary and unjustified. They are wrong because the accompanying hardship, powerlessness and monotony can shatter personal esteem and confidence. They are wrong because they are borne not by some mythical, subhuman underclass but by ordinary human beings, by parents who struggle to do the best for their children. The inequalities are wrong also because, for the advantaged, they can engender a greed which makes them intent on accumulating more and more despite the fact that this entails others having less and less. A divided society.

Like Erica, I desire a more equal society. By this, I do not mean that everyone should be identical clones. Rather it is a society in which the distribution of resources, opportunities and responsibilities do not weigh the odds so heavily against one section of the population that they are channelled into much greater likelihood of social distress, poor housing, restricted environments, under-achievement, unemployment, ill-health and even premature deaths, than the rest of the population. In short, it is a society in which the differences between the seven writers in this book and the privileged élites highlighted by the newspaper cuttings are distinctly narrowed.

If nothing else, the contributors to this book should convince others that those who have low incomes, who experience many social traumas, who live in council estates and inner cities, are not poor by their choices or by their just deserts. Despite their disadvantages, they can still struggle, can still love their children, can still participate in neighbourhood projects, can still have views and can still write. If only the powerful politicians would listen, if only the wealthy professors would understand, if only the media moguls would open their pages to them, if only Christians would put beliefs into practice. If only they would have faith in the poor.

*Notes*
1. Rowntree Foundation, 'The future of work', Summary No. 7, February 1996.
2. Rowntree Foundation, 'Expenditure on children in Great Britain', Findings No. 118, July 1997.
3. A. Rogers, cited in *The Observer*, 11 June, 1993.
4. R. Pryke, *Taking the Measure of Poverty*, Institute of Economic Affairs, 1995, pp. 68, 95.
5. F. Bennett (ed.), *Out of Pocket: Failures of the Social Fund*, Family Welfare Association, 1996.
6. R. Wilkinson, *Unfair Shares*, Barnardo's, 1994.
7. C. Murray, *The Emerging British Underclass*, Institute of Economic Affairs, 1990.
8. D. Gittins, *The Family in Question*, 2nd edition, Macmillan, 1993.
9. B. Holman, *FARE Dealing: Neighbourhood Involvement in a Housing Scheme*, Community Development Foundation, 1997.
10. R. Whelan, *The Corrosion of Charity*, Institute of Economic Affairs, 1996, p. 80.
11. B. Jordan, *Social Work in an Unjust Society*, Harvester/Wheatsheaf, 1990, p. 3.
12. Social Services Inspectorate, *Better Management, Better Care*, Stationery Office, 1997, pp. 2, 9.
13. B. Holman, *A New Deal for Social Welfare*, Lion Publishing, 1993, p. 75.
14. M. Wroe, 'The British believe in... not putting bums on pews', *The Observer*, 9 November 1997.
15. J. Thomson, 'The everyday lives of service users and social welfare workers: a materialist analysis', PhD thesis, University of James Cook, 1997.
16. R. Wilkinson, *Unfair Shares*, p. 68.
17. B. Holman, *Towards Equality: A Christian Manifesto*, SPCK, 1997, pp. 81–84.

18. R. Lupton, *Return Flight,* Family Consultation Service Urban Ministries, 1993.
19. P. Henderson, *Social Inclusion and Citizenship in Europe,* Opbouwcahier, 1997, p. 22.
20. P. Mandelson, *Labour's Next Steps: Tackling Social Exclusion,* Fabian Society, 1997.
21. Rowntree Foundation, 'Expenditure on children'.
22. R. Lister, *The Exclusive Society: Citizenship and the Poor,* Child Poverty Action Group, 1990, p. 72.
23. B. Holman, *FARE Dealing.*
24. P. Mandelson, *Labour's Next Steps,* p. 3.
25. A. Goodman, P. Johnson and S. Webb, *Inequality in the UK,* Oxford University Press, 1997.
26. B. Holman, *Towards Equality,* pp. 118–20.
27. *The Guardian,* 18 November 1997.
28. *The Guardian,* 5 and 14 November 1997.
29. *The Guardian,* 20 October 1997.
30. *Daily Mail,* 24 September 1997.
31. *The Guardian,* 19 September 1997.
32. *The Guardian,* 22 August 1997.
33. Advertisement in *Life Magazine,* 26 October 1997.
34. *The Guardian,* 12 November 1997.

# Bibliography

Anderson, D. (ed.), *The Kindness That Kills*, SPCK, 1984.

ATD Fourth World, *Talk With Us, Not At Us*, Fourth World Publications, 1996.

Bennett, F. (ed.), *Out of Pocket: Failures of the Social Fund*, Family Welfare Association, 1996.

Beresford, P. and Turner, M., *It's Our Welfare: Report of the Citizens' Commission on the Welfare State*, National Institute of Social Work, 1996.

Beresford, P., Stalker, K. and Wilson, A., *Speaking for Ourselves*, Social Work Research Centre, University of Stirling, 1997.

CES, *Outer Estates in Britain: Easterhouse Case Study*, Centre for Environmental Studies, 1985.

Gittins, D., *The Family in Question*, 2nd edition, Macmillan, 1993.

Goodman, A., Johnson, P. and Webb, S., *Inequality in the UK*, Oxford University Press, 1997.

Green, R., *Community Action Against Poverty*, Kingsmead Kabin, 1997.

Harrison, D., 'Why Glaswegians prefer to slum it', *The Observer*, 31 October 1993.

Henderson, P., *Social Inclusion and Citizenship in Europe*, Opbouwcahier, 1997.

Holman, B., *A New Deal for Social Welfare*, Lion Publishing, 1993.

Holman, B., 'Shaken not stirred', *The Guardian*, 22 January 1994.

Holman, B., *FARE Dealing: Neighbourhood Involvement in a Housing Scheme*, Community Development Foundation, 1997.

Holman, B., *Towards Equality: A Christian Manifesto*, SPCK, 1997.

Hutton, W., *The State We're In*, Jonathan Cape, 1995.

Jordan, B., *Social Work in an Unjust Society*, Harvester/Wheatsheaf, 1990.

Lister, R., *The Exclusive Society: Citizenship and the Poor*, Child Poverty Action Group, 1990.

Lupton, R., *Return Flight*, Family Consultation Service Urban Ministries, 1993.

Mandelson, P., *Labour's Next Steps: Tackling Social Exclusion*, Fabian Society, 1997.

Massie, A., column in the *Glasgow Herald*, 13 November 1988.

Murray, C., *The Emerging British Underclass*, Institute of Economic Affairs, 1990.

Pacione, M., *Glasgow*, Wiley, 1995.

Pigott, R., 'The executive exodus', *The Guardian*, 24 September 1997.

Pryke, R., *Taking the Measure of Poverty*, Institute of Economic Affairs, 1995.

Rogers, A., cited in *The Observer*, 11 June 1993.

Rowntree Foundation, 'The future of work', Summary No. 7, February 1996.

Rowntree Foundation, 'Expenditure on children in Great Britain', Findings No. 118, July 1997.

Social Services Inspectorate, *Better Management, Better Care*, Stationery Office, 1997.

Tawney, R., *The Attack and Other Papers*, Allen & Unwin, 1981.

Thomson, J., 'The everyday lives of service users and social welfare workers: a materialist analysis', PhD thesis, University of James Cook, 1997.

Whelan, R., *The Corrosion of Charity*, Institute of Economic Affairs, 1996.

Wilkinson, R., *Unfair Shares*, Barnardo's, 1994.

Wroe, M., 'The British believe in… not putting bums on pews', *The Observer*, 9 November 1997.